EVERY STEP
ADVENTURES WITH JESUS

EVERY STEP

ADVENTURES WITH **JESUS**

40 DAYS OF
GUIDED PRAYER

Erika DeJonge

Every Step: Adventures With Jesus
Copyright ©2023 by Erika DeJonge

All rights reserved. No part of this publication may be reproduced, stored in a retrieval system, or transmitted in any form or by any means, electronic, mechanical, photocopying, recording, scanning, or otherwise, except as permitted under Section 107 or 108 of the 1976 United States Copyright Act, without the prior written permission of the Publisher. Requests to the Publisher for permissions should be sent to Erika DeJonge at embeelen@gmail.com.

Scripture quotations marked (NLT) are taken from the Holy Bible, New Living Translation, copyright ©1996, 2004, 2015 by Tyndale House Foundation. Used by permission of Tyndale House Publishers, Carol Stream, Illinois 60188. All rights reserved.

Scripture quotations taken from the (NASB®) New American Standard Bible®, Copyright © 1960, 1971, 1977, 1995, 2020 by The Lockman Foundation. Used by permission. All rights reserved. lockman.org

Scripture quotations marked (NIV) are taken from the Holy Bible, New International Version®, NIV®. Copyright © 1973, 1978, 1984, 2011 by Biblica, Inc.™ Used by permission of Zondervan. All rights reserved worldwide. www.zondervan.comThe "NIV" and "New International Version" are trademarks registered in the United States Patent and Trademark Office by Biblica, Inc.™

Scripture quotations are from the ESV® Bible (The Holy Bible, English Standard Version®), © 2001 by Crossway, a publishing ministry of Good News Publishers. Used by permission. All rights reserved. The ESV text may not be quoted in any publication made available to the public by a Creative Commons license. The ESV may not be translated in whole or in part into any other language.

Scripture quotations taken from the Amplified® Bible (AMP), Copyright © 2015 by The Lockman Foundation. Used by permission. lockman.org

Scripture quotations marked TPT are from The Passion Translation®. Copyright © 2017, 2018, 2020 by Passion & Fire Ministries, Inc. Used by permission. All rights reserved. ThePassionTranslation.com.

Published in the United States of America
ISBN: 9798871164266

Cover and Interior Design by Gloria Erickson, London Lane Designs and Julia Arambam

Dedication

I dedicate this book to my son, Logan, and his future siblings. May your adventures with Jesus be far greater than I could ever ask or imagine. May my stories launch you into the wild wonder of the One who made you and called you by name. And may my Jesus stories pale in comparison to yours.

Table of Contents

Foreword	1
Acknowlegments	3
Introduction	5
Prologue	9
Chapter 1: A Surrendered Heart	17
Chapter 2: Eager to Hear	21
Chapter 3: Trusting God to Break Barriers	27
Chapter 4: Trusting God to Provide	33
Chapter 5: Walking in Obedience	39
Chapter 6: Inviting God In	43
Chapter 7: God's Undeniable Goodness	49
Chapter 8: Saved, Healed, Delivered	53
Chapter 9: Fresh Eyes for Scripture	57
Chapter 10: The Power of Forgiveness	61
Chapter 11: Living Intentionally	65
Chapter 12: Pursuing God-Given Passions	71
Chapter 13: The Gifts of the Spirit	75
Chapter 14: Our #1 Calling in Life = Loving God	79
Chapter 15: Pursuing Justice	85
Chapter 16: Complete Dependence	91
Chapter 17: Surrender, Sacrifice, and Suffering	95
Chapter 18: The God of Miracles	97
Chapter 19: Freedom from Unforgiveness	101

Chapter 20: Bringing Shalom to Chaos	105
Chapter 21: The Wedding at Sinai	109
Chapter 22: A Call to Radical Hospitality	115
Chapter 23: Iron-Sharpens-Iron Community	119
Chapter 24: Learning to Worship	123
Chapter 25: Sabbath Rest	127
Chapter 26: Celebrating God's Faithfulness	131
Chapter 27: Choosing Joy in All Circumstances	135
Chapter 28: Pondering God's Favor	141
Chapter 29: God Always Trades Up	147
Chapter 30: Freedom From Striving	151
Chapter 31: Praying for Healing	157
Chapter 32: I AM More Than Enough	161
Chapter 33: He's a Good, Good Father	167
Chapter 34: God Sees Our Every Need	171
Chapter 35: Praying With Intention	175
Chapter 36: Interview Time	179
Chapter 37: A Surprise from the Holy Spirit	183
Chapter 38: An Epic Surprise	187
Chapter 39: Hearing God's Voice	193
Chapter 40: My Challenge to You	197
Epilogue	201
About the Author	203
References	205

Foreword

I didn't want to write this book, but I promised God I would always listen and obey. He promised to lead and guide me every step of the way. I had already promised God I would obey, so when He said I should write a book, I listened, and here we are.

This book is simply a compilation of my adventures with Jesus. It is not intended to bring any shame or condemnation if your adventures look any different. It is simply my story of walking with God and learning to listen and obey while I pursue knowing Him more and more. I share these stories in hopes that you'll see God more often in the details of your everyday life and expect Him to speak more today than you did yesterday. In Revelation 19, we're told that the testimony of Jesus is the Spirit of prophecy. I believe if Jesus has done it for me, He'll do it again, and He'll do it for you! So please, if nothing else, let these stories open your mind to what God wants to do, not only in my life but in yours, too. May these stories and questions lead you to ponder new things with God, and may your walk with Jesus always be filled with wonder and adventure!

Acknowledgments

Thank you to everyone who called, texted, emailed, and supported me emotionally, prayerfully, and financially during my three years in Nepal. Thank you to everyone who visited and stood with me from a distance. A special shout-out to Engedi for being such a great sending church and to Megan Herzog (member care advocate), who loved and supported me so thoroughly during my time in Nepal and my transition back home. I also want to thank all the Spirit-filled people I encountered in Nepal who opened my eyes to "the more" of God: Olivia Watkins, Matt Gibson, Glenda Hauser, my beloved BFANepal ladies, BFANepal interns, and short-term teams. And to my husband, Andy, thanks for supporting me in this book-writing journey and for committing to going with me on all the adventures yet to come.

Many people reviewed and edited this book, and it wouldn't be what it is today if it weren't for them. Thanks, Mom, for editing everything I've ever written. Also, thanks to Jessica Irvin, Megan Herzog, Olivia Watkins, Kelly Isham, Heather Morse, and Gloria Erickson.

Introduction

Erika sacrificed many things to move to Nepal. She laid down the expectations she had for her future and surrendered her life to go where the most excellent Father was calling her. We make these sacrifices knowing He is worth it, always worth it, but even being here myself has not made her sacrifice any less inspiring. Erika's love for God is evident in how she lays herself down for others. It is evident in the way she hears God call her to the secret place, and she runs to Him. It is clear in the beauty that radiates from this woman inside and out. She is beautifully crafted in the image of her heavenly Father, and in spending time with her, there is no mistaking that beauty and its pricelessness.

Erika took three years to be a marker of God's hand moving in Nepal, but no matter where she goes, she will bring that presence with her and transform lives as she goes. She has loved extremely well, serving people with her time, attention, and affection. I know the ladies of Beauty For Ashes Nepal (BFANepal) have felt truly loved and known by her. For three years, she intentionally stopped on every floor in our building to greet everyone at the beginning of each workday. She has prayed with the women, talked through difficult things with them, offered medical advice and vaccinations when needed, and shared many meals with them. She has poured into the people in this business and ministry and loved them well while also loving other missionaries working here—people whose families are thousands of miles away and who sometimes just really need a babysitter. She has cared for their children, brought them meals, celebrated American holidays with them, helped them move, and has been present when they needed her.

She has not just loved all these people well; she has also loved me really well! The truth is, I don't think I could have taken on the role of Executive Director of Beauty For Ashes Nepal if she had not been here. My training for this role was brief, and this was by far the most significant leadership position ever entrusted to me. I felt the weight of responsibility as I stepped into my new role. As I looked around at the business, I was overwhelmed by the changes we needed to make quickly to get back on track with government regulations and bring order and growth to our organization.

Erika was a huge key in stabilizing the business during a rocky transition. She had already spent two years investing in creating systems for things like shipping, customer communications, and invoicing. She knew what we had done as a ministry and as a business in the past, and she also had wisdom concerning how to move forward in the future. I am confident God placed her here at a strategic time to give us what we needed so that one day, we would be safe to move forward even without her. If she had not been here, I may have resigned, but because she was here, I knew that I was not in this alone. She encouraged me and took each step with me, even when things felt like they were piling up. I always knew there was someone to bounce ideas off of and speak correction if I had gone too far or needed to stand taller and be more confident in what I was doing. She gave me these priceless gifts as a friend, co-worker, and mentor.

I learned so much from Erika over my two years working beside her. Because of her investment in BFANepal and because of her investment in me, I felt more capable of standing in my role even as the desk beside me became empty. She taught me values surrounding communication, relationships, and organization, and those things have stayed here in Nepal even though she is gone. The love she poured into me, our ladies, and many others also remain, and Erika will not be forgotten. In some ways, I can say I don't know what we will do without her because she brought a sense of community to this office that is lacking without her. But in another sense—and perhaps a higher compliment to who she is—we will continue to move forward well because of the groundwork she laid for us. She helped stabilize us when we were shaking in the growing pains of transition, but now, as she is gone, we will hold still and be all the better for the time she was a part of our community and family here in Nepal.

Sincerely,
Olivia Watkins
Former Executive Director
Beauty For Ashes Nepal

Prologue

Unfortunately, I was somehow raised in the church, grew up reading the Bible (God's Living Word), studied countless examples of God speaking directly to humans by giving them dreams, visions, and prophetic words, and somehow still missed the fact that God wanted to speak to me each and every day. Can you relate?

Thankfully, before leaving for Nepal, I was given a book called *God Guides* by Mary Geegh. (I highly recommend this book as it dramatically shaped how I hear from the Lord today.) If you don't run out and buy the book today, I'll summarize it. Mary was a missionary in India. Basically, for every issue that came up, for any person who came to her seeking advice or help, her solution was always the same. Here's paper and a pencil; let's sit in silence until the Lord speaks to us. Once He speaks, we'll do whatever He says. That's seriously the entire book, but she has a plethora of incredible testimonies of how Jesus spoke, how they did the unexpected thing Jesus said, and how it solved their problems. Again, you should read it.

God Guides provides a wide array of testimonies that will increase your faith that God wants to speak to, lead, and guide you. The book inspired me to go on a journey of learning to hear from God so that I, too, could listen and obey. I hope this book will give you tools so that listening and obeying feel less daunting. I'd like to take you on a journey with Jesus. I pray that as you ponder with Jesus through guided questions, listening and obeying will become comfortable and familiar, maybe even second nature.

One Wednesday, I was enjoying a Sabbath at home alone with Jesus. Nurses work the weekends, so I would take every Wednesday as my day off. I also fasted from food every Wednesday as a way of living out my desperation for Jesus. So, I had read several of Mary's testimonies and decided, okay, I'm going to try this out for myself. I'm going to listen and obey.

I sat there with my paper and pen and waited for my word from the Lord. The first thing that came to mind was, *"Get up and eat."* I promptly told God, "No, sorry, but it's Wednesday. You know I'm fasting today." Again, I heard, *"Get up and eat."* I again corrected the Lord, "No, I'm fasting today. I can't eat." *"Aren't you hungry?"* Came the response in my head. "Of course I'm hungry!?! I haven't eaten all day!" *"If you won't obey me when I tell you to do what you want, how will you ever obey me when I ask you to do something you don't want to do?"*

Touché, Jesus, touché'. I got up, ate, and tried to refrain from correcting Jesus from that day forward.

Now, using paper and a pencil is just one way to stop, look, and listen to God. I'm not about to venture into making an all-inclusive list of all the ways God can speak to us. The important thing to remember is that the more we seek Him, the more ways He speaks.

To get things started, I want to highlight a few basics I believe every believer should be aware of. It's not rocket science, but communication with our Father God can certainly feel like a foreign language. But trust me, He's very patient in the process. And He promises in John 10:27, *"The sheep that are My own hear My voice and listen to Me; I know them, and they follow Me"* (AMP).

Five of the ways I believe we can hear from God today:

1. **His still, small voice.** It's often the first thought that pops into your mind. I say "pops" because you can't trace back logically to where it started—it just popped into your mind out of nowhere. People often argue with, "But it sounds the same as me thinking," and it's true. It's not a booming, audible voice of the Lord, but thoughts that were not your own that just popped into your mind. I agree. It'd be easier if a loud, booming voice came through every time I asked a question. But alas, His ways are higher than my ways, and He doesn't often choose to speak that way. I'd propose that He's checking to see who has a strong desire to hear from Him.

2. **Feelings/Impressions.** Sometimes, you can get an overwhelming sense of joy or peace while praying. Sometimes, while praying over someone, you can feel fear or anxiety out of nowhere—giving you a hint of how to pray for them. These can be God speaking through your heart language. For example, when I was called to Nepal, my heart had an unexplainable peace that never wavered. I just *knew* in my heart of hearts that I was called to Nepal, and that was okay. In reality, I had NEVER wanted to move abroad. I'd never dreamed of being a missionary. There

were people who disagreed with me about my call to Nepal and tried to talk me out of it, but my heart had an unwavering peace that told me I was walking in the right direction. God speaks to our heart in ways only our heart understands. My heart had a confidence I couldn't wrap my head around.

3. **Artistic expression.** I have never been one to dabble much in the arts, but creating with Jesus can be a beautiful way to allow Him to speak to you. I've never independently created a piece of art that anyone but my mother would hang on their fridge, but creating with Jesus is a different story! Somehow, when I allow Jesus to direct the paintbrush, my flowers are identifiable instead of blobs on a page. When working with wounded women in Nepal, we used art therapy as a way to allow them to express pain and then ask Jesus to reveal His perspective and healing presence. Invite Jesus into your creative process—get paper and colored pencils out and imagine with Jesus. Paint with Him, dance with Him, practice photography with Him. Let Him guide you. He might just surprise you!

4. **Pictures/Images.** The first time someone prayed over me and said, "I see a picture of you ..." I imagined they closed their eyes and saw a massive, bright billboard with a message on it. That has not exactly been my experience. Can you picture your living room couch? Can you describe it to me? What color is it? What style is it? Everyone can picture their living room couch. It's in that same brain space the Lord can show you pictures. I love to ask, "Jesus, please show me a picture of how you see me today." His

perspective is so life-giving and encouraging! At first, it can feel so faint that you're not sure it's really there, but if you keep asking questions, you'll surprise yourself as you can actually describe what you see. The key is then to ask Jesus questions: Why are you showing me this? What do you want me to know about this image? What are You trying to communicate to me through this picture? Ask Him questions. He loves to engage in conversation with you and share His heart with you!

5. **Bible Verses.** The Lord speaks through His written Word. In my quiet times, I've asked the Lord to speak and have heard a Bible reference, looked it up, and discovered it spoke directly into a situation I had been praying into. There are other times when practicing with friends that I received Malachi 5:8. I quickly discovered there are only four chapters in Malachi, so you don't always hit the nail on the head. But the point is, you're trying to hear from God, and I believe He shows up where there is faith. A child doesn't quit trying to walk because he falls down. No, he gets up and tries again, as should we.

Speaking of missing the mark, you should always practice discerning if what you're hearing is from God. Here are a few questions you can ask about what you're hearing, seeing, or feeling:

1. Is it in line with the Word of God? God's word for today will never go against His written Word.
2. Is it in line with God's character?
3. Do Biblical mentors agree?
4. Does it resonate with your spirit? Does it sit right in your heart?

Ponder with Jesus

This is the part of the book where you sit down with Jesus, ponder together, and practice hearing Him speak to your heart. I beg you not to skip this portion—it can feel scary at first, but we serve a Good Father who desperately wants to speak to you! And please, don't feel you must answer every question in every pondering section. These are just ideas to get you started. Use the ones that speak to you and skip the ones that don't.

Let's start practicing. I know that might sound overwhelming, but I promise I'll walk you through it step-by-step. Trust that God wants to speak to your heart today!

Pray and ask the Lord to speak. Pray something like, "Father God, Jesus Christ, and Holy Spirit, I long to hear from You today. Please come and clear my mind of any distractions and speak to me. Please forgive me for not seeking to hear Your voice more often. I repent of any lies I believe that say You don't want to speak to me or that I can't hear You. I cling to the truth that You want to speak to me today, and You have given me ears to hear. Please open the eyes and ears of my heart and help me see and hear clearly from You today."

Then pray aloud, "Jesus, please show me a picture of how You see me today." Then stop, look, and listen. Do any thoughts pop into your mind? Look with the eyes of your heart in that space where you can picture your living room couch. Do you see any images there? If so, ask Him more questions: Why are You showing me this? What do You want me to know about this image? What are You trying to communicate to me through this picture? Check in with your heart–how are you feeling? Are you feeling suddenly loved, joy-filled, or peaceful?

If the Lord spoke something to your heart today, write it down, even if it was faint. Trust that the Lord spoke to you and cling to whatever He said. If you don't feel like you heard, saw, or felt anything, dwell on the truth that the Lord wants to speak to you. Declare it as truth over your life. Open your heart to the fact that He WILL start speaking, and you want to be ready to hear. Try not to be discouraged; the journey may take time, but it will definitely be worth it! Thank the Lord for the fact that He wants to speak to you and for the journey you're about to go on.

Chapter 1
A Surrendered Heart

And without faith it is impossible to please him, for whoever would draw near to God must believe that he exists and that he rewards those who seek him.

~Hebrews 11:6 ESV

I vividly remember sitting in a comfortable, air-conditioned church service in Holland, Michigan, when my local church announced its goal to send out 60 mid- and long-term missionaries in the next five years. I remember thinking, "That's a huge goal! I don't feel called to go, but I have a solid income as a nurse; I'll help write the checks!" Never in a million years did I imagine I would be one of the people hopping on a plane. Nevertheless, for as long as I can remember, I have always told Jesus, "I'll follow You wherever You lead. I'd rather not be a missionary, but You know I would never tell You no. But really, nursing is my mission field, right?"

Growing up, I recall sitting at countless Christian conferences where people were called to missions, and I was always thankful it wasn't me. I never wanted to have those awkward support-raising coffee dates. I never wanted to leave my friends and family. But I always had a heart of surrender. I often wondered why our lives looked so different from the lives of the disciples. I spent my spare time discussing with friends what it could look like to live differently. What are we called to as Christians? I always wanted to live for Jesus and to live intentionally, but I never thought it'd be on the mission field. I was bound and determined to figure out what it looked like to love and pursue Jesus with all of my heart. I had cried out to Jesus countless times, "I'm desperate for more of You, Jesus." As it turns out, that's a prayer He always answers with a "Yes."

Ponder with Jesus

Before we move on, I have to ask. Is your heart in a place of complete surrender? Before we go on this journey together, are you willing to be all in? If not, are you willing to be made willing? Sometimes, when I don't have enough faith for something God is asking me to do, I just pray that simple prayer: "Lord, help me be willing to be made willing." Is your heart softened before the Lord? Or are there things you hold tight that you'd never give up for Jesus?

Spend some time asking the Lord to bring to mind any areas of your life that you need to surrender. Whatever comes to mind, surrender them. If you're not there yet, ask Him to help you be willing to surrender. Seriously, do it now. He's worth it, I promise. This book is full of testimonies of God speaking, moving, and astounding me. But don't take my word for it. Ask Jesus to show you that He's worth it.

Practice listening for His voice by praying, "Lord, please show me an image that confirms in my heart that You are worth it all. Surrender feels hard; please show me Who I'm surrendering to and that You're worth it." Then stop, look, and listen. What do you hear, see, or sense?

Also, commit right now to surrendering this journey to the Lord. Commit to reading this book from start to finish—not just reading it, but engaging on the journey God has for you. I promise, no matter where you are on your journey with God, He has more He wants to give you!

Pray with me: "Lord, I surrender this journey to You. Any walls in my heart that need to be demolished, I give You permission to tear them down. I want to know You more at any cost. I want to experience You more tangibly in my life. Please open the eyes of my heart and speak to me today and every day. I love You and can't wait for more adventures with You. Amen."

Chapter 2
Eager to Hear

Therefore, as the Holy Spirit says, "Today, if you hear his voice, do not harden your hearts as in the rebellion, on the day of testing in the wilderness,"

~Hebrews 3:7-8 ESV

In eighth grade, I knew I wanted to be a nurse when I grew up. I wanted to love and serve people in their darkest hours and be the hands and feet of Jesus to those who needed it most. I graduated from high school, attended the University of Michigan, and got my bachelor's degree in nursing. I was a nurse for about two and a half years in Ohio and then moved back home to my beloved and beautiful Holland, Michigan, so that I could begin my career in the Pediatric ICU (PICU). When I accepted the position in the PICU, I was confident that it was my dream job; it would be a perfect fit, and I'd be a PICU nurse for a long, long time.

God, however, had different plans. About a year into my job in the

PICU, I started feeling restless, angsty, and bored. Occasionally, I would have weeks where I absolutely loved my job, but the average day became long and slow, and I began to feel like there had to be something more. So, I sought the Lord, "God, what's next for me? You must have something more for me. The PICU cannot be what You have in mind for me long-term! What's next?" I felt God say, *"Just wait."* So, a week or two later, I'd ask again, "God, what's next?" And again, I felt in my spirit, *"Just wait."* This became a bit of a cycle and one week, I replied, "God, I'm sick of waiting! What's next?" *"Just wait until Nepal."* came the response this time. Now, talking to God felt comfortable and familiar, but hearing God respond to me was pretty unfamiliar territory, yet I felt sure God had spoken to my heart.

I had already signed up for a two-week, short-term trip to Nepal through my local church, and we were scheduled to leave in about a month. I figured I could wait that long. So, I quit asking for more details. But as I prepared for my trip to Nepal, I felt God opening my heart to global missions. I remember telling multiple friends, "I feel like God's opening my heart to global missions, but that's just crazy. I'm a nurse, I've always been called to be a nurse, I have zero desire to be a missionary, but God's doing something."

It finally came time to go on the trip, and I was eager to get there and see what God wanted to do. I remember landing in Kathmandu, Nepal for the first time and walking around the capital city of about a million people and just thinking, "Man, I could never live here." It was hot, dirty, dusty, smoggy, crowded, and chaotic. Did I mention it was HOT? I'm more of a small-town girl who loves the solitude and beauty of hiking and the beach. I also greatly appreciate air conditioning. Kathmandu had none of the above!

But our team of about twelve people quickly left the capital city for the foothills of the Himalayas, and suddenly, we were out in nature with hills, trees, rivers, and so much natural beauty! It was an incredible week of trekking. We would hike all morning and part of the afternoon, doing countless numbers of stone steps as we climbed up and down hills and valleys. Then, we'd get to a village and engage the local people in spiritual conversations. We even got to share the Gospel with people that had NEVER heard of Jesus. It was truly an incredible week!

Throughout the week, while hiking for hours on end, I enjoyed asking each of my teammates what they were passionate about. People will talk forever about things they are most passionate about—giving me a chance to listen (and breathe). But then they would turn and ask me what I was passionate about. So, I spent quite a bit of time sharing with people how I was passionate about helping women exploited by the sex industry but that I was struggling to get involved in the States. I felt a burden for this group of women, but my life didn't really reflect my passion–yet.

Well, our week of trekking through the beautiful, rugged countryside of Nepal came to an end, and we found ourselves back in Kathmandu. I remember talking to my roommate, the only other girl on the trip, and my newfound best friend; we both agreed that although the village life in Nepal was beautiful, we were not a fan of Kathmandu, and we were SO ready to escape the crazy, chaotic city by hopping back on a plane! Kathmandu was simply not the place we wanted to settle in and get comfy.

Our last day in Nepal was a Sunday morning, and I vividly remember waking up with two things on my mind. Number one,

"God, I came to Nepal, but You still haven't spoken." This was extra surprising to me because I normally feel God's presence more easily in nature. We had been hiking in nature ALL week, and no direction had come!?! And number two, "We have GOT to get to church today!" I just had this burning desire to get to church that came out of seemingly nowhere. Unfortunately, church was not on the schedule as we planned to take a flight to view Mount Everest, shop for some souvenirs, and debrief our trip. So, I told my roommate, Megan, "I think we should convince the team to go to church today." She was all for it! Well, the flight to Everest went incredibly fast, with no delays and no traffic jams (shocking for Nepal). And we found ourselves eating breakfast with enough time to still get to church. So, we convinced our team full of men that shopping wasn't important and we should definitely go to church. Thankfully, the men were on board with cutting the shopping trip short, so, we went to church.

We were sitting in a church service that we weren't supposed to attend, and Megan and I ended up sitting right behind Glenda, the director of Beauty For Ashes Nepal (BFANepal). We learned that BFANepal is a jewelry and accessory manufacturing company that works to employ women who have been rescued from the sex industry. I was getting excited as we were talking with her. I asked, "What is your greatest need? How can we help?" She looked directly at me and said, "Honestly? We need more volunteer staff to come and serve long-term." And in that moment, the Holy Spirit grabbed hold of my heart.

Throughout the worship time, we sang songs about surrendering completely to God. I truly felt the Holy Spirit working to help me surrender all of my wants, desires, plans, and rights over to God.

Then, the entire sermon was on Hebrews 3:7, "Today, if you hear His voice, do not harden your hearts" (ESV). And then, I knew without a doubt that God had spoken directly to me and was calling me to Nepal long-term.

When the service ended, we continued our conversation with Glenda, and I remember telling her (with a face full of shock and disbelief, I'm sure), "I think God just called me to move here and work with you!?!" I was shocked, yet confident, that the Lord had spoken.

We then went to have lunch as a team and debrief the trip. I remember sharing with my team, "Yeah, um, I think God just called me to move here and work with Beauty For Ashes long-term!" I remember our guide telling me, "Whatever God spoke to your heart today, write it down and stick to it! You'll get back to America, and people will tell you you're crazy, and you'll start to question what you heard. Life will get busy, and it will be easy to forget what God said. So, whatever He said today, write it down and stick to it!" And so, I did. I wrote it down, and I stuck to it.

Ponder with Jesus

I just have to ask: do you believe that God still speaks today? No, seriously, do you believe the Creator of heaven and earth, Almighty God, wants to speak to you today? Do you believe He cares about you enough to talk with you? God is the same yesterday, today, and tomorrow. He spoke to the Israelites, He spoke to His prophets, He spoke to His disciples, He spoke through a donkey, and He wants to speak to His children still today. I promise.

But will you listen? Take some time to reflect on your life. Is your prayer life full of you telling God updates and asking for things? Or is it a two-way conversation? Our God is relational, and He wants a personal relationship with you. Last time I checked that requires two-way conversations. Please believe me when I tell you God still speaks today. He wants to speak specifically into your life. He wants to lead and guide you. He wants you to stop and listen and gain His perspective on your situation. Are you open to hearing from Him?

Take a moment to repent for not taking enough time to listen for His voice. Pray something like, "Father God, I repent of being so busy living my life and asking You to help with things that I haven't taken the time to tune my ears to hear from You. I repent of believing the lie that You don't value me enough to speak to me or that You're too busy to communicate with me. I'm sorry for being so caught up in my own needs and desires that I haven't stopped to ask for Your input. Please help me change and go in a new direction today. Please open the eyes and ears of my heart. Please help me learn to listen and obey."

Then practice. Pray aloud, "Lord, what's one truth You want me to know today?" Then stop, look, and listen. What do you see, hear, or sense? Do any thoughts pop into your mind? Do any images flash before the eyes of your heart (where you can picture your couch)? How is your heart feeling? Whatever you're noticing, ask the Lord questions. "What do you want me to know about this picture?" "Why is my heart feeling this way?" Explore with the Lord and trust that He's speaking to your heart!

Chapter 3
Trusting God to Break Barriers

So here's what I've learned through it all: Leave all your cares and anxieties at the feet of the Lord, and measureless grace will strengthen you.

~Psalm 55:22 TPT

So, after my sudden and surprising call to missions and debriefing our trip as a team, we hopped on a plane back to America. We arrived home the following evening, and I immediately sat my parents down at the kitchen table and plainly told them, "I'm pretty sure God just called me to move to Nepal and work with Beauty For Ashes long- term." The shocked looks on their faces reflected what I had initially felt in my heart. Are you sure? How is this possible? But you just moved home a year ago? You're a nurse; why would you give that up? There's human trafficking here in West Michigan;

why do you need to move halfway around the world to fight for justice? These, among other things, were topics of conversation that evening, but then my Mom brought up a really valid question, "What about your narcolepsy?"

Narcolepsy is a sleeping disorder which gave me an extreme tendency to fall asleep at inappropriate times. I was diagnosed in 2008, my freshman year of college, and have been on tightly controlled stimulants ever since. Here's a sneak peek into my life with narcolepsy...

After eight motionless hours of sleep, the fourth alarm clock rings, and I awaken to find three missed alarms! It's now or never. I guess my morning quiet time will get missed again today—time to get up. Oh, but it's an epic battle to even throw back the covers. And once I finally muster up the energy to get my feet planted on the ground, I start my day feeling half-awake. The first thing I do is take my "stay-awake drugs" and attempt to get ready quickly despite still feeling like I'm the walking dead. I rush out the door and pray I don't fall asleep on the road. With the music cranked to try to stay awake, I head for work in the PICU. Thankfully, work is the least likely place for me to fall asleep.

The overwhelming desire for a nap sits at the forefront of my mind throughout the workday, but I know it's just not an option. Occasionally, I'll squeeze in a quick rest at lunchtime if I can escape the unit. I try to keep busy and avoid sitting down to ensure I'm awake and alert. It would be detrimental if I missed the downward trends in my critically ill patients. I take more drugs at lunchtime to avoid the otherwise inevitable post-lunch snooze. If I am lucky, the day can pass surprisingly fast from busyness. But I always take more drugs around dinner time to ensure I'm awake enough to drive home safely after a twelve-hour shift.

Sometimes, I'll call people on my thirty-minute drive home to help ensure I don't doze while driving. Even if friends are hanging out, I generally head home to avoid falling asleep while socializing—I've been told it's quite rude. Once I get home, I attempt to find the energy to unpack my lunch and maybe get something done, but more often than not, I end up sitting down to hang out with my family and fall asleep before ever making it to bed.

Days off from work look slightly different in that it's less critical for me to stay awake. I'll often start my day with a workout, then sit down to read and have quiet time with God. Generally, quiet time turns into an epically long nap time in no time at all. The struggle is all too real.

Why do I share this with you? Because this was an average day while taking my meds—which helped drastically. It turns out the drugs that helped me stay awake were unavailable in Nepal. They were also tightly controlled in the U.S. and were restricted to a thirty-day supply at a time. In Nepal, there are no mailing addresses, so getting my meds delivered to me every thirty days was just not feasible.

When God called me to Nepal, narcolepsy was one of the first barriers I identified. I told multiple people, "God's not going to call me to Nepal just to sleep 19 hours a day!" Without meds, I was barely functional and could literally sleep the entire day away! I told God right away that if He wanted me to move to Nepal, He had to provide a way for me to stay awake once I got there. So, I surrendered the barrier completely over to Him and totally quit worrying about it.

I had an appointment with my sleep doctor, talked to her about my move to Nepal, and inquired about potential overrides on the standard thirty-day supply limit. She said she would look into it and email me any options she discovered. When she emailed me, I was super busy, so I glanced at it and left it in my inbox for a few days. Every time I went to read the email, I felt convicted. *"Just trust. Just trust".* So, I left the email alone for a few more days. Later, when I went to deal with the email, I again felt God saying, *"Just trust Me."* So, I deleted the email without ever reading it.

That night, I was talking with a friend at the beach and told her that I felt like God was asking me to trust Him to take care of my narcolepsy. The next morning, I woke up to an email from Glenda, the Director for BFANepal. Her email said I should get in touch with Gwen, their designer, who was temporarily in the States for a few months. She said I'd be blessed by her story because she had been healed from narcolepsy while serving in Nepal. God's timing is just impeccable.

I contacted Gwen, and she invited me to attend her open house at her church in Detroit. So, two of my closest friends and I took a quick road trip to Detroit that Thursday evening. It was such a blessing to be able to talk with someone else who had been working and living in Nepal. I was encouraged by the work she had been doing and her willingness to share about her struggles with narcolepsy and how she was healed while living in Nepal. Both Gwen and her mom prayed over me for healing. We shared hugs, and my friends and I hopped back in the car for our three-hour drive back to Holland.

The next morning, I woke up to my first alarm, hopped out of bed, and started to get ready. And it hit me. I'm WIDE awake! I don't feel like a zombie! I feel AWAKE! Praise God!!! So, I threw my "stay-awake drugs" in a drawer without taking any and proceeded to work out with Megan. Then I had a quiet time and didn't fall asleep! And for the rest of the day, I did multiple activities that would previously have resulted in a guaranteed nap, but I didn't nap once!!!

For the first few drug-free days, I still felt tired at times, but I'd pray, and the fatigue would pass. When day four came around, and I still did not need my meds, I could say without a doubt that I had been healed!

Narcolepsy no longer has a hold on my life! I wake up each morning without the epic battle I had become so accustomed to. I can have extended quiet times without dozing. I can drive without worrying about falling asleep. I can spend time with friends at any point of the day without passing out. And most importantly, I can give all the praise and glory to God! For eight years, I depended on drugs to keep me awake enough to function. For years now, I have remained drug-free and have been more awake than ever before! I feel like I have so much more time and have spent most of my extra time reading and spending time with God. It's been so great knowing I can actually have a quiet time with God instead of missing out because of never-ending exhaustion.

The most encouraging part to me is how clearly God was paving the way for me to move to Nepal. He knew far in advance that I would need Him to conquer this barrier. And He proved Himself faithful once again! As I moved forward with my plans to move to

Nepal, I knew without a doubt that God had incredible things in store. AND I could be confident that I'd be awake to take part in them! Praise God!!!

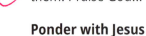

Ponder with Jesus

Is there a barrier in your life that you need to hand over to God AND TRUST that He will handle? What does it look like to rest in His goodness instead of striving to make everything work out? He has supernatural solutions to all of our earthly problems, and He's working all things out for the good of those who love and serve Him. We often miss out on miracles because we're bound and determined to find our own solutions. What's the Lord asking you to release today?

Stop, clear your mind, and ask, "Lord, please bring to mind a barrier I'm facing in my life right now." When it comes to mind, ask God, "What does it look like to hand this barrier over to You?" Then stop, look, and listen. What are you seeing, hearing, or sensing? Did any random thoughts pop into your mind? Look into that space where your living room couch easily appears. Do you see anything? If so, ask the Lord questions. "Jesus, what do You want me to do with what You're showing me?" Then, do whatever He says. Practice resting in His goodness today after handing over the stress of striving.

Chapter 4
Trusting God to Provide

Keep your lives free from the love of money and be content with what you have, because God has said, "Never will I leave you; never will I forsake you."

~Hebrews 13:5 NIV

As I spent five months wrapping up my life in Michigan and preparing to move to Nepal for three years, God consistently provided for my every need. I continued to learn to completely depend on Him, and He continued to be faithful!

The last week before I left for Nepal, however, the journey seemed to get really hard, really fast. The goodbyes became filled with tears instead of smiles, and reality set in. I was leaving! I was leaving my friends. I was leaving my family. I was leaving my church. I was leaving my vast community and solid support system. I was leaving my beloved Holland, Michigan, and the shores of Lake Michigan.

I would no longer live with my brother and sister-in-law and their three adorable kids, who always seemed to know when I needed hugs and snuggles. I was no longer going to be two blocks away from my parents. I was no longer going to be able to have family dinner every Monday night at my parent's house. I would no longer have my best friends available at any hour of the day for coffee, workouts, or hikes. Things were about to change...drastically.

But God is Faithful. And God continued to be faithful to provide for my every need. God loves to provide for us physically, financially, emotionally, and spiritually.

For example, financial support had been steadily rolling in over the prior few months, but in the weeks leading up to leaving, I was still pretty far from my goal. I had sent out exactly one mass email asking for monetary support at the beginning of the summer, feeling called to simply trust that God would provide. I didn't feel called to strive to raise support and waste my summer worrying about money. Well, over the final few weeks before leaving, my trust dwindled, and I decided to just settle for less than my original support goal. I rationalized that God wasn't providing it all because my first housing situation was fully furnished, and a lot of the anticipated up-front cost was setting up an apartment. I figured if I ran short later, I would pursue support-raising from Nepal. When people asked how support-raising was going, I told them I was "funded enough to leave."

Thankfully, God had a different idea! He wanted me to know that He is faithful, I am His daughter, and He will provide beyond what I could even ask or imagine! Before I left, God astonished me with the generosity of my community, and I was reminded, once again, that God is loaded! Just two weeks before I left, I received a $6000 check from a distant friend who hadn't even asked how support-raising was going. I also received a few other donations that got me to my goal, and all this after I had lost faith that all the money would come in before I left. I was absolutely astounded by God's goodness! I "knew" in my head that God is faithful and capable of providing for my every need, but to experience His abundant provision so clearly and just before hopping on a plane spoke to my heart that God is faithful and trustworthy. I'm so thankful God knew how to speak to my heart so I could trust Him more fully. So, I was able to leave in full confidence, knowing that God had and would continue to supply my every need! My expected expenses for the first year were met—without my striving or worrying. It turns out God is absolutely capable, even without my help!

But God doesn't just care about me physically. He also cares about me on an emotional level! There were over 60 people who came to show their love, encouragement, and support one Friday night at my going-away party. Never in my life had I felt so blessed, supported, and uplifted by the community of believers around me. That night was filled with encouraging words, fun, food, fellowship, and laughter. My community also paused the celebration to spend time in prayer for me, my friends, my family, and my future community in Nepal! As I prepared to leave, God was so incredibly faithful to provide for me emotionally!

But God doesn't only care about my physical and emotional needs. He cares about my whole being. He took care of me spiritually through a conference two weeks prior to leaving that refreshed and renewed my relationship with Him. The conference was three full days and called The Power of Prayer. I had a wonderful time communing with God and enjoyed being at a level of intimacy that had gotten lost in all the busyness of moving to a third-world country. After the conference, I had a renewed sense that God speaks when we take the time to listen. And He was saying, *"Come, follow Me. I will never leave or forsake you!"*

So once God had filled my cup to overflowing—physically, emotionally, and spiritually, it was time to go. It was time to surrender everything I had and everything I was. It was time to hop on the plane. Ahh! I felt like I could relate to Peter taking those first steps out of the boat and onto the water, "God, the task in front of me is too great! I am not able!" (Matthew 14:22-31). But instead of focusing on the waves crashing in, I chose to cling to the promise that He is faithful! He is faithful! He is faithful!!!

Ponder with Jesus

How are you doing when it comes to trusting God? Are you depending on him physically, emotionally, and spiritually? Or are you striving to make things work on your own? If things are tight financially, are you striving to make ends meet? Or are you praying and trusting for a miracle? God wants to show up for you! Are you burned out emotionally? God wants to renew your strength. Are you spiritually dry? God wants to encounter you; He promises to draw near to those who draw near to Him.

Is God asking you to step out of the boat? Ask the Lord, "What's one step You want me to take this week?" Then stop, look, and listen. Is there any area of your life coming to mind where God is asking you to set down your fears, put on some courage, and walk with Him? Ask Him, "What's one thing You want to give me this week?" Then stop, look, and listen. Where God guides, He provides, so trust He'll grant you what you need to do the hard things. Repent of anything standing in your way and then decide you're going to take that step of faith... and DO IT!

Chapter 5
Walking in Obedience

Bless the Lord, O you his angels, you mighty ones who do his word, obeying the voice of his word! Bless the Lord, all his hosts, his ministers, who do his will!

~Psalm 103:20-21 ESV

I was a nurse—I thought—although my daily life suddenly looked far from anything I had ever imagined. If we're being honest, I never thought I'd move away from my beloved Holland, Michigan, ever again. I never thought I'd enter the world of business as a mission. And I certainly never thought I'd move to a developing country and work as the Assistant Director of a wholesale jewelry and accessory manufacturing company. But God is hilarious, comes up with these silly plans, and then is faithful to see them come to fruition.

So, there I was, suddenly in Nepal, less than six months after He said to go. Some people labeled me a missionary (that term initially made me super uncomfortable). Others called me crazy for leaving my dream job with a steady salary, 401k, and health insurance. Certain individuals said I was selfish to leave my parents and family to worry about my safety. A few people remarked that I was lucky to travel the world and go on a grand adventure. But really, I was just another person doing life with Jesus, going where He directed.

I was living in Nepal doing what I had always done. I was following God's call on my life. God called me to study at the University of Michigan for a season. Next, I followed His leading to Ohio, where I spent my days nursing in the hospital. As that chapter came to an end, I let Him guide me back to Holland to continue my journey as a nurse in the PICU. Then, I followed His lead to work with BFANepal. I was always about obedience. He did not view one job as more or less. I was serving Him just as much as a nurse as I was as a missionary. The same goes for you—you don't have to be a missionary overseas to walk in obedience. You do, however, need to listen and obey.

Life in Nepal was different, but my perspective didn't change. Listen and obey. It's that simple. As children of God, when we ask with expectation, He will answer us! I turned into a nurse working in a jewelry and accessory business. I knew pretty much nothing about running a business and even less about jewelry, but there I was, walking in obedience. I quickly learned that true obedience requires a great deal of dependence on the One who sent me.

For example, just six weeks after I arrived, the Executive Director of Beauty For Ashes left for a two-month furlough in the States, leaving me to manage the business in her absence. After just six weeks in the business, I was suddenly in charge of directing designers on what to create, managers on how much product to make, as well as communicating with customers to ensure they were up to date and satisfied with their orders. I remember feeling oh-so ill-prepared, so vulnerable, and untrained. Six weeks in a developing country is barely long enough to learn where and how to buy your groceries! And here I was, running a business employing over twenty women with less than six weeks of training. I could barely count my Nepali money, and here I was, managing orders in two currencies! It felt absolutely crazy. But it was in those early days that I learned what it meant to trust God in *everything*: the big picture things, like leaving family and friends behind for three years, as well as the small details, like which particular type of bracelet should be designed today. Honestly, I remember looking at a sheet a designer handed me of potential bracelets and just praying that the Lord would highlight one because I was absolutely clueless and was expected to give direction. I can't say that the bracelets designed that day made us millions, but I can say that I learned to trust God in the process, in the details, and I learned to trust that He would lead, guide, and direct my steps (big or small) when I ask Him to lead. I was practicing, literally every day, what it meant to listen and obey.

Ponder with Jesus

So, let me ask you, have you ever considered what it looks like to listen and obey? When was the last time you asked God what He wanted to do with your life? Are you following the call He's placed on your heart? Because God created you with a purpose, and He longs for you to ask Him what that purpose is! What if you're missing out on the extraordinary plans God has for your life because you're too comfortable, busy, and distracted by your daily life to ask?

Here's a great opportunity to stop, look, listen, and ask aloud, "Jesus, what was I created for?" Believe in your heart that He wants to reveal your purpose to you. Then stop, look, and listen. Write down anything you hear, see, or sense, and take time to reflect on it. Are you walking in obedience? Are you walking in your purpose?

If you don't happen to hear, see, or sense anything, ask the Lord to reveal anything standing in the way of you being able to hear Him. If He brings something up, ask Him to deal with it. If it's a wall, ask Him to break it down. If it's a lie standing in your way, ask Him for the truth instead.

If you're still not receiving from Him, take some time to reflect on what is special about you that God would want to partner with. (Examples: serving, creating, worshiping, following, etc.) And try not to get discouraged; the Lord is faithful, and as we tune our ears to Him, we will hear Him more and more.

Chapter 6
Inviting God In

Hear my prayer, O Lord; let my cry come to you! Do not hide your face from me in the day of my distress! Incline your ear to me; answer me speedily in the day when I call!

~Psalm 102: 1-2 ESV

My daily life in Nepal was just a little different than my average week in the States, so I'll attempt to draw you a quick picture of my new normal. The sun and barking street dogs woke me up around 6:30 am, and I would enjoy a peaceful morning in the arms of Jesus—reading the Bible, praying, journaling, worshiping, etc. I would then grab a quick breakfast and head out the door with my roommate. We walked for about ten minutes through the winding, dusty streets of Kathmandu (half of which always seemed to be under construction). Occasionally, we would find ourselves rock-climbing on our way to work over and around piles of rocks, gravel, and sand for the next road, home, or store that was being developed. Detours were never posted, and it seemed that anyone could create a construction project at their leisure despite large inconveniences to others in the area. On an average day, there was usually some sort of adventure involved in our commute.

Once we got to the main road, we would hop on a bus that was going in the direction of work. There was no bus schedule, rhyme, or reason to the buses; we just hopped on one that was going in the right direction. Keep in mind that people carried a wide assortment of things with them on the bus, not excluding their sleeping or screaming babies or live chickens. Sometimes, we would even see goats riding on the racks on top of the buses. Pretty much anything was fair game if it needed to be transported. Then, we would get off five minutes later and hop on another bus that took us to the road that BFANepal was on. This whole journey took anywhere from 30 to 45 minutes, depending on how long it took for buses to come our way, how many cows were holding up traffic in the street, or how many street dogs we had to dodge. For someone with a core value of efficiency, life in Nepal was quite stretching—no systems or rules, no stop signs, traffic lights, or road signs. It sure kept us on our toes!

Once we arrived at work, we could take a breath of fresh air. BFA felt a little bit more American inside, with less chaos and more aesthetically pleasing artwork and systems. The workday started with devotion time, which included everyone in the business—generally 25 Nepali women and three Americans. Our Nepali managers all spoke English and would translate into Nepali so everyone could participate. Devotion time varied quite a bit, but regardless of who was leading or what it looked like, the workday started with focusing on Jesus first and foremost, no matter how many orders we had waiting for us to complete. Then we went our separate ways and would go to our respective jobs. The women would either head to the offsite metal-smithing office, the jewelry floor, or the sewing floor. And the Nepali managers and a few of us foreigners would head to the office floor to get to work.

From about 10 am to 5 pm, Glenda (the Executive Director), my roommate, and I worked at our computers to keep the business running smoothly. A highlight of the day was eleven o'clock when chiya (milk tea) was served to each of us. It was warm, smooth, full of sugar, and absolutely delicious. Nepali culture is very communal, which often meant chatting over a cup of chiya–we were more than happy to participate in this cultural experience! Lunch was another highlight. BFA provided lunches for all of our employees. In Nepal, "If you haven't eaten rice, you haven't eaten." So, most days included rice of some kind. Dal Bhat, pressure-cooked lentils over rice, is the meal most Nepalis eat twice a day, every day. Regardless of what was served to us, we enjoyed eating it together, braiding each other's hair, painting each other's nails, threading each other's eyebrows, and just enjoying our thirty minutes to relax and build community together–the best we could across the language barrier.

After work, we'd hop two buses back home, work out, eat dinner, shower, and then get on with our evening activities. Evenings generally consisted of more quiet time, video calls to loved ones back home, Bible study, movie nights, or social activities with other women from church. Sounds like the typical week in America, right?

I think the most beautiful part of my job in Nepal was the freedom we had to put God above business. There were times when we were in the middle of processing important financial documents, and someone would come to us needing prayer, wisdom, or encouragement. We immediately stopped and ministered to them. Every time, no questions asked! It made me think back to life as a nurse, and I wonder how many times I missed opportunities to stop and pray. There were times we would be in the middle of working on a spreadsheet, and we'd get stuck. We would literally speak aloud, "Jesus, please show us how to fix this." And you know what? He came through with a solution nearly every time!

Ponder with Jesus

How different would your workday look if you walked each step in complete dependence on Him? What if you invited God into your daily life? No, really...every area of your life! What if, in every conflict that arose, you asked God what He wanted to reveal to you? What if, with every issue at work, you turned to God first and your own knowledge second? What if every time you didn't know how to discipline your child, you asked God to show you and teach you the way? God answers us when we ask with expectation. We simply need to stop, look, and listen for His answer!

Are you making space in your life to listen? When you hear His voice, are you ready to obey? Stop and think of a problem you're facing in your life. Whatever situation comes to mind, invite God to speak into it. He has supernatural solutions for every earthly problem you're facing.

I love to ask God questions. "Lord, please show me Your perspective on this situation. Jesus, please show me a picture of how You see this person. Holy Spirit, what's the next step You want me to take? Father God, what do You want me to do with what You've shown me today? Abba, please show me a picture of how You see me today. "

Pick a couple of the questions above and ask the Lord. Then stop, look, & listen. What is He showing you? Are you seeing, hearing, or sensing anything? What is He whispering to you? Now go and obey.

Chapter 7
God's Undeniable Goodness

I remain confident of this: I will see the goodness of the Lord in the land of the living.

~Psalm 27:13 NIV

God is good...All the time. All the time...God is good.

We've all heard this countless times in church, but it recently hit my heart more fully. I think so often, when hard times come, we are so quick to ask, "Why would a good God let such terrible things happen?" I think God wants us to ask questions and get to know Him better, but I often think we're asking the wrong questions.

If God is still on trial in our hearts—if it's not settled if He's good or not, then we don't fully grasp the Good News of the Gospel! John 15:13 says, "Greater love has no one than this, that someone lay down his life for his friends" (ESV). Our God sent His Son to die for us—there is no greater love. Our God died for us—there is NO greater love! Regardless of what life throws at me. Regardless of the trials or bad days that come my way. No matter what God asks me to sacrifice. No matter how long a difficult season lasts. My God is good!

There was a season during my time in Nepal when it felt like chaos was circling around me. Within a month or two, I had close friends struggle with a miscarriage, friends choosing to live in unrepentant sin, friends not receiving visas to stay in Nepal, family members needing multiple surgeries, unresolved conflict in close relationships, and other difficult things in seemingly every direction.

Now, I could have spent all of my mental energy focusing on the problems and chaos all around me. I could have spent countless hours questioning God about why He'd let these things happen or why He didn't prevent them. I could even question God on whether or not He's even good—if He were a good God, why would He allow these things to happen?

Instead, I chose to renew my mind by focusing on the truth of His Word (Romans 12:2), that God is Good and He will never leave or forsake me! No matter how big the problem, my God is bigger. The enemy was defeated, and my God is King. I know how the story ends, so I won't waste my time and energy putting God on trial. I know in my heart of hearts that He is Good, and His love endures forever.

Instead, I learned to ask questions that allowed God to speak into my life. Psalm 139:23 says, "Search me, O God, and know my heart; test me and know my anxious thoughts" (AMP). I believe God wants us to ask Him to search our hearts and speak into our lives. What areas of sin and weakness do You want to reveal to me? What am I supposed to be learning about You through these trials? What area do You want me to grow in during this season? How can I better love You and others during times of testing? What does it look like to love well in this situation?

Suddenly, God is good again as He uses difficult times to grow and shape us into sons and daughters! And as we step into who we were created to be, He's excited to use us to bring His Kingdom on earth as it is in Heaven! He is never on trial anymore because He has played His trump card—sending His Son to die for us—there is no greater love!

Ponder with Jesus

So, are you feeling the heat of the refining fire? Are you in the middle of trials and tribulations? If so, which questions are you asking? Is God still on trial in your heart? Or can you trust in the goodness of God in ALL circumstances?

Spend some time with the Lord, repenting of any accusations you've thrown His way. Pray Psalm 139:23-24, "God, I invite your searching gaze into my heart. Examine me through and through; find out everything that may be hidden within me. Put me to the test and sift through all my anxious cares. See if there is any path of pain I'm walking on, and lead me back to your glorious, everlasting way—the path that brings me back to you" (TPT). Ask aloud, "Lord, please bring to mind any lies I believe about You." (That He's not inherently good or trustworthy, that He has ulterior motives, or He wants to cause you pain.) Then, repent of partnering with any of the lies that came to mind. "Lord, I repent of partnering with the lie that _____." Then, give the lie to Jesus and ask Him for His truth in return. "Jesus, I hand You the lie that _____, what truth do You want to give me in return?" Then stop, look, and listen. What is the Lord speaking to your heart?

If you don't hear, see, or sense anything, or even if you do, reflect on His goodness. Spend some time worshiping Him for who He is—A good, good Father.

Chapter 8
Saved, Healed, Delivered

She will give birth to a son, and you are to give him the name Jesus, because He will save His people from their sins.

~Matthew 1:21 NIV

One day, we had special visitors from No Boundaries International come to BFANepal to do some inner healing ministry with our staff. They were incredibly gifted, anointed ministers who brought the presence of God with them. They had medical knowledge and background but had found Jesus to be the best medicine and/or therapy ever prescribed. Their ministry wasn't super complicated, but it was super effective in bringing freedom through the cross of Christ.

Inner Healing might be a new term for you. So, let me expand. The Greek word "sozo" means saved, healed, and delivered. As Christians, we believe that Jesus came to save us from our sins, but I believe He did so much more than that. Isaiah 53:5 says, "But he was pierced for our transgressions, he was crushed for our iniquities; the punishment that brought us peace was on him, and by his wounds we are healed" (NIV).

Therefore, I believe the Lord's desire is for us to be not only saved from our sins but also healed and delivered, not only in heaven but also here and now. How can I be so sure? Jesus Christ taught His disciples to pray, *"Your Kingdom come ... on earth as it is in heaven"* (Matthew 6:10 NIV). We know with confidence that we will be healed and whole in heaven, so why shouldn't we join Jesus in praying, "Your Kingdom come, on earth as it is in heaven," right now?

The ministry time with our ladies included asking Jesus to bring to mind a time, memory, or situation that needed to be restored. The leaders then encouraged the ladies to draw a picture of what came to mind. Next, they were to invite Jesus into the situation and ask Him where He was during those difficult times. It was an incredible time to let Jesus speak peace into horrible situations and turn them into peace-filled memories. It was incredible to watch Jesus bring more freedom to the BFANepal ladies. And I believe He has more freedom in store for each and every one of His sons and daughters.

Ponder with Jesus

What are your thoughts? Do you believe Jesus has more freedom for you here on earth? Or do you believe you'll need to get to heaven to be saved, healed, and delivered? I believe God has more freedom available for you here and now!

Ask the Lord, "Please bring to mind a memory You want to heal." Then stop, look, and listen. Fully immerse yourself in whatever memory comes to mind. Immerse yourself in what you were feeling at that moment. Allow your heart to feel the pain of that moment. Then, ask the Lord, "Please reveal Your presence to me in that moment." Then stop, look, and listen. Do you see, hear, or sense anything? I pray the Lord is revealing His healing presence to you in that moment and healing your heart of the pain of that memory. As you connect with Him in that memory, ask Him to heal your pain. Ask Him any questions that are burning in your heart. Allow His presence to overwhelm you and fill you with His peace and comfort. Sit with the Comforter for as long as you'd like. He promises to comfort the brokenhearted.

Chapter 9
Fresh Eyes for Scripture

All Scripture is God-breathed and is useful for teaching, rebuking, correcting and training in righteousness, so that the servant of God may be thoroughly equipped for every good work.

~2 Timothy 3:16-17 NIV

One day, I was pondering the Bible with a friend—something we frequently did throughout my time in Nepal. I struggled to understand something my friend was saying because it was so different from what I had been taught growing up. I remember him asking, "Is that what scripture says? Or is that what you were taught?" And it hit me: I had been reading the Bible expecting to see certain things and glossing over other things that I didn't have a framework for. I'll forever remember our conversation that morning because it resulted in me removing (to the best of my ability) the preconceived notions I had about what scripture said, and it invited me into reading the Bible for myself. From that day forward, I asked the Holy Spirit to come and teach me what He wanted me to know.

For me, it made everything so much clearer. I had always wondered why the Bible said, "Do not get drunk on wine," (Ephesians 5:18 NIV) but I still had Christian friends getting drunk. I couldn't understand why the New Testament talks all about living in the power of the Holy Spirit, healing the sick, feeding the poor, and taking care of the widows and orphans. Yet, we were all more concerned about paying off student loans and saving for retirement than feeding the poor or healing the sick. We were ill-equipped and quite uncomfortable with walking in any of the gifts of the Spirit.

From that day forward, I've attempted to read the Bible for myself with the guidance of the Holy Spirit. And then, to the best of my ability, I do what it says! Crazy, I know. I'm incredibly thankful that I was raised in the church, went to Christian schools, and grew up being quite familiar with scripture. However, it's prideful to think that one denomination's theology has it all figured out or that one person or teacher could hit every nail on the head. So, there are things that I was taught growing up that were right on point, but there are other things that were omitted or taught in a way that misled my beliefs that the Lord later helped me see differently.

Ponder with Jesus

What about you? Have you read the Bible for yourself? Does the Bible have supreme authority in your life? Do you do what it says to the best of your ability? Have you tried reading the Bible for yourself, cover to cover, and asked the Holy Spirit to guide you through it? If not, I highly recommend carving out the time to study the Bible with fresh eyes and fresh ears. But for today, we'll ask the Lord where He wants to start.

Pray with me, "Lord, please remove my lenses of expectations of what scripture should say and open my eyes and ears to hear what You want to tell me." Then pray aloud, "Lord, please bring to mind a Bible verse You want to show me today." Then stop, look, and listen. What comes to mind? If you hear a verse, look it up. Read it. Ask the Lord, "What do You want me to know about this verse?" Listen for the Lord to speak to your heart. There might be a topic the Lord wants to clear up. There might be a chapter of the Bible He wants you to start with. There might be an area of sin you've been struggling with. There might be a fresh truth He wants to show you. Whatever you hear, see, or sense, dwell on it and chew on it for the rest of the day. The thing with God is there's always more. I believe we'll receive greater revelation of who God is for all of eternity! Let's start now!

Chapter 10
The Power of Forgiveness

And whenever you stand praying, if you find that you carry something in your heart against another person, release him and forgive him so that your Father in heaven will also release you and forgive you of your faults. But if you will not release forgiveness, don't expect your Father in heaven to release you from your misdeeds.

~Mark 11:25-26 TPT

What's the first thing that comes to mind when I say Christmas? Forgiveness? Yeah, me neither, but my first Christmas in Nepal was a beautiful, joy-filled experience where repentance and forgiveness were highlighted during our staff Christmas party.

Although outside, it felt like just another day in Kathmandu, as Christmas is not a nationally recognized holiday in (primarily Hindu) Nepal; inside the walls of BFANepal, the joy was palpable as we sang and danced for our Lord. Celebrating Christmas with the staff was unlike anything I had ever experienced! In America, I often got bogged down by the materialism of our culture during the Christmas season. There are so many things to distract us from the true hope and joy that comes through the Baby in the manger. But in Nepal, I had the privilege of sharing Christmas with women who were celebrating their first Christmas ever–women who, just one year prior, had never experienced the joy and freedom of the Lord!

We enjoyed playing the "Secret Angel" game (like Secret Santa) in December. The ladies absolutely loved trying to trick each other and joke around about who their secret angel might be. The joy and laughter were incredible as the final reveal happened during our staff Christmas party. My cheeks literally hurt from smiling and laughing so much. The party started with a brief reminder of why we give gifts on Christmas—because God first gave His only Son as a gift to us. We then had a time of asking for forgiveness for any hurts we had caused in the last year and spent time in prayer together. It was beautiful because one of our Nepali managers led the devotion on forgiveness and then publicly asked for forgiveness in specific areas where she had failed. Starting the party with absolute humility led to others openly repenting and clearing the air. Never before had I been to a Christmas party that included publicly asking for forgiveness, but in Nepal, I was reminded that there is so much more to Christmas than fun, food, and fellowship. It was just so beautiful!

After thinking about it, it makes a lot of sense. Christmas was a key play in God's story of forgiveness. Without Christmas, we don't have Easter. Without Easter, there is no grace and forgiveness for all our sins. Without repentance and forgiveness, we miss out on the incredible gift of God's wholeness, freedom, and complete healing that He bought for us on the cross!

It's interesting that we talked about forgiveness during Christmas because unforgiveness is one of the greatest barriers to connection—with God or others. When we refuse to forgive, we harbor unforgiveness and bitterness, which wreak havoc on our relationships, our heart, and our health. If we choose a life of forgiveness, we choose to pursue the fullness of God's peace, joy, and freedom. But it's just that—a choice! Will you choose forgiveness?

You could say that Christmas in Nepal was the stripped-away, more Christ-centered version of Christmas. I felt absolutely honored to celebrate Christmas with each one of the women. The peace, love, joy, and hope that comes through the story of Christmas is truly life-changing! Have you let it thoroughly change your life?

Ponder with Jesus

Forgiveness is a choice, not a feeling. The verse above states that if we refuse to forgive our brother, we tie God's hands, and He's no longer able to forgive us! Think about that for a second. Do you want to jeopardize your freedom, peace, and joy? Do you want to have barriers between you and Jesus? Or do you want all lines of communication as open as possible?

Pray aloud, "Lord, please bring to mind anyone I need to forgive today." Then stop, look, and listen. Then pray aloud, "Lord, is there anything I need to forgive myself for?" Then stop, look, and listen. What's the first thing that comes to mind? Even if you think you've forgiven completely, if Jesus brings it up, forgive. If in doubt, choose forgiveness.

Whoever and whatever God brings to mind, forgive them. Right now. Marianne Williamson says, "Unforgiveness is like drinking poison and expecting the other person to die." There's no offense too big, too numerous, or too grotesque for God to forgive, and as image bearers of Christ, we are expected to walk in the same grace and forgiveness as our Lord.

Speak out your forgiveness. "I forgive (name) for (offenses). I choose to forgive them and release them completely from all of their offenses. I choose to bless them and their children. I hand them to You, Jesus, and pray You would move powerfully in their life." Repeat as many times as necessary.

Now, go walk in freedom!

Chapter 11
Living Intentionally

Here I am! I stand at the door and knock. If anyone hears my voice and opens the door, I will come in and eat with that person, and they with me.

~Revelation 3:20 NIV

The devil likes to use busyness to distract us from what is truly important. It's ridiculous how easily intentional time with Jesus gets replaced with work, meetings, social engagements, sleep, and traveling. How quickly we grow distant from the Lord as His voice gets drowned out by the craziness of our busy schedules. How quickly we turn to friends instead of the Lord when we have a long week or an exhausting day.

Pursuing Jesus is an active, not passive, activity. I've learned that unless I block out intentional time to spend with Jesus, it just doesn't happen. I've always known this to be true, but somehow,

Erika DeJonge

I expected it to be easier on the mission field. Unfortunately, it was the same struggle. When the alarm went off in the morning, I still had to resist the snooze button and make the choice to get up and start my day with Him. Unfortunately, the snooze button was just as tempting in Nepal as it was back in the States. On occasion, I'd go through a couple of weeks of struggling to hear God's voice clearly. I'd realize, once again, that without intentionally building into my relationship with Jesus, I had been falling back into old habits of doing life on my own, under my own plans, and by my own strength, and that is exhausting. Thankfully, He's quick to respond when I finally press in and return to a place of complete dependence on Him and His guidance!

Pursuing Jesus requires intentionality and often looks different to different people or in different seasons. I know for me in Nepal, sometimes I needed to get out of the chaotic, busy, crowded, smoggy city to find fresh air and waterfalls and reconnect with what God was saying. Sometimes, the busyness of running a business, hosting short-term mission teams, and maintaining connections with people back home would crowd my schedule and my mind, and I'd just have to step out of the city to reconnect with the One who made me and called me.

Sometimes, I needed to take intentional rest time alone with Jesus. My roommate and I had what I called "no pants days." In Nepal, shorts were considered immodest, so to go outside, pants were required. Our little flat felt like such a refuge, and outside often felt so foreign, chaotic, and hard. So frequently, on Saturdays, I'd declare a "no pants day," which meant I was literally not leaving this flat. Because I need to rest, I need to be alone with Jesus in my bedroom, and I just refuse to face the brokenness of this world until I'm reminded of the goodness of God. And the Lord met me in that flat.

At other times, I felt called to put myself in knowingly awkward situations because it meant building relationships with the people I went to serve. Even after three years of living in Nepal, I often felt like I was just one move away from a giant social faux pas. You don't realize how many cultural differences are unexplainable until you live in another culture. You can go through all the cultural classes in the country and still find unwritten rules and social expectations that, as a foreigner, you can just straight up miss. So, it was often easier to withdraw at work and just eat with the other foreigners serving there. But I would try my best to be intentional with the opportunities in front of me, and I would try to be intentional in eating lunch with the Nepali ladies–even though there was always the fear of social suicide, the dread of attempting to communicate in a language in which I could barely grocery shop. I knew I wasn't called to Nepal to be comfortable. I knew I was called to Nepal to love the ones in front of me. And so, I tried. Was I successful 100% of the time? Absolutely not, but being intentional about eating with the Nepali managers every Monday or the jewelry girls once a week, for example, definitely helped me build connections much faster than if I had just stuck to what was comfortable.

I was also privileged to help my roommate grow in her discipline and intentionality. Liv (Olivia) once shared that she felt like God was asking her to practice discipline and get up at 5 am every day. Without much thought, I offered to join her on the journey. She was shocked and felt so loved. I didn't think much of it as I was accustomed to early morning workout dates in America, but that January started our journey of getting up at 5 am every day to work out, shower, and have an hour with Jesus all before work. This sounds great, but I forgot to mention that in Kathmandu in January, it's about 35 degrees Fahrenheit inside your room at five in the morning. So, we had to be VERY intentional and incredibly disciplined to crawl out of our cozy beds to ensure we had time to take care of our mind, body, soul, and spirit before work, but the payoff was so worth it! We both grew in discipline, and Jesus definitely met us on many of those cold, cold mornings. Then we could go to work and pour out of our overflow from Jesus filling us up in the early morning hours.

Throughout my time in Nepal, God grew my desire and capacity to live intentionally. We do not naturally become closer to God, become better evangelists, or fluent Nepali speakers. If we want to improve our situation in life, we need to take action and be intentional! None of this is new information, but it's good to be reminded that good things come to those who are willing to put in the time and effort while pursuing God's calling on their lives.

People often say they are too busy to have daily quiet time with Jesus. The reality is you have time for what you make time for. If you believed daily time with the Lord was important, you'd put it first and foremost in your day, and anything and everything else would fall in line behind it. Don't believe me? Try it for a week. I'm always amazed by how much I accomplish in a day when I give the first portion to the Lord. It's like He multiplies my time or makes me super efficient the rest of the day. It's like tithing—He can do more with 90% than I can do with 100%. Similarly, He can do more with 23 hours than I can do with 24! Try it out—you'll be amazed at how much you can do with your day when you give the first portion to Him! Start with 15-20 minutes a day and work up from there.

He is totally worth it! And I dare say you can afford a little bit less time on social media or watch one less episode on Netflix and still survive the day. Hey, you may even find that your perspective on life improves when you feed your mind with His Word instead of consuming the media this world offers.

Ponder with Jesus

Are you creating space for Jesus in your daily life? How do you connect with Jesus? Are you creating space to spend time with Him daily? Are you giving Jesus space to guide and direct your steps each day? Jesus promises to draw near to those who draw near to Him. Are you intentionally drawing near? Or are you doing your own thing and asking Him to bless it? Take an honest look at your schedule. Would a third-party person know that you love Jesus by looking at your schedule? Or is time with Jesus an afterthought? If the Creator of heaven and earth wants to spend quality time with you, will you prioritize Netflix over Him? Be honest with yourself and God; are you intentional with your time?

Ask the Lord for tangible next steps. Each time you sit down to spend time with the Lord, ask Him, "Jesus, what do You want to do today?" And then stop, look, and listen. It's such a simple way to practice hearing from Him. It might not be a booming response, but you may feel more inclined to pick up your Bible vs. your journal vs. the book you've been reading together. Or the Lord may bring you to a particular Bible verse or bring a certain someone to mind for you to pray for. He might encourage you to write a note to someone, or He might help you cross unimportant things off your list for the day. It's such a great way to spend time with Him—you're showing Him your love by giving Him your time and attention, and He reveals more of Himself to you, leading to greater connection and intimacy. Try it! Be intentional, and make the time. He's SO worth it!

Chapter 12
Pursuing God-Given Passions

For we are God's handiwork, created in Christ Jesus to do good works, which God prepared in advance for us to do.

~Ephesians 2:10 NIV

I believe it's important to discover what you're passionate about and then set aside time to invest in those passions. God crafted each of us with a particular set of gifts and passions, with assignments for each of us to carry out during our time on this earth.

From a young age, I knew I was called to love and serve people in their darkest hours. For a while, that looked like nursing. Then I moved to Nepal, and I loved women who were transitioning out of some of the most horrifically dark hours you or I could imagine. I discovered that loving and serving people in their darkest hours can look different in different seasons. But my passion never changed. I just put down the syringes and medications and picked up invoicing and procuring raw materials. It's the heart behind what you're doing that matters so much. I don't believe every Christian is called to the mission field. I do, however, believe every Christ follower is called to bring His Kingdom on earth as it is in heaven—that can be on the mission field, in the hospital, at the office, on Wall Street, at home raising children, etc. The important thing is to be where God wants you and to carry His presence while doing it.

While in Nepal, I discovered that I'm passionate about beauty—creating, experiencing, enjoying, and capturing beauty! My time in Nepal was full of great adventures as I attempted to escape the chaos of the city to find beauty anywhere and everywhere. Beauty in the city was often hidden by busy streets, polluted air, and barking dogs, so pursuing beauty was more of a challenge than it was back home.

One weekend, a few months into my time in Nepal, I went to a village a few hours out of the city with a friend from my hometown who just happened to be living in Kathmandu for four months. We went to stay with her host family at their parent's home in the village. I was blown away by the beauty of God's creation just three hours away! I literally cried when we found the waterfall—if I closed my eyes, it felt like I was on the shores of Lake Michigan. I have always connected with God through the beauty of His creation, so it felt like a little taste of heaven. God is good at loving us in the details—loving us how we need to be loved.

Ponder with Jesus

What about you? What are you passionate about? What are you doing with your time? Are you pursuing your God-given passions?

Or are you binge-watching Netflix and continuously scrolling through social media? Are you intentionally setting aside time to work toward the things God gave you a heart for?

What can you do this week to intentionally discover and pursue your God-given passions? Think and pray about it. Ask God, "What am I passionate about? Have I lost sight of anything I used to be passionate about? Where do you want me to invest my time? What do I need to cut out to give more time to my passions?"

Or maybe you've been pursuing your passions but have left Jesus out of the picture? Invite Jesus into the things you're passionate about. If you absolutely love photography—how can you use photography to invest in His Kingdom? Whatever you're pursuing, invite Jesus in. Ask Him to breathe life into your passions and reveal to you how they fit into His Kingdom's purposes. You guessed it—Then listen and obey!

Chapter 13
The Gifts of the Spirit

For example: "The Spirit gives to one the gift of the word of wisdom. To another, the same Spirit gives the gift of the word of revelation knowledge.

And to another, the same Spirit gives the gift of faith.

And to another, the same Spirit gives gifts of healing.

And to another the power to work miracles.

And to another the gift of prophecy.

And to another the gift to discern what the Spirit is speaking.

And to another the gift of speaking different kinds of tongues.

And to another the gift of interpretation of tongues.

Remember, it is the same Holy Spirit who distributes, activates, and operates these different gifts as he chooses for each believer."

~1 Corinthians 12: 8-11 TPT

Erika DeJonge

About six months into my time in Nepal, Glenda (BFANepal's Executive Director) and I hosted a conference called the Open Heaven Conference. We had an international prophetic ministry team that came to host conferences in two different cities in Nepal. It was an incredible time of hearing from the Lord about His desire to see His kingdom come on earth as it is in heaven. There was also incredible worship time, prophetic activation, people receiving the baptism of the Holy Spirit, people receiving the gift of tongues, personal ministry time, and people being miraculously healed. We finished the week off with an epic worship and dance party!

Of all the incredible things that happened throughout the week, I think my favorite part was when two guys from Scotland, Neil, and Euan, took the kids out for a children's program. They taught about the prophetic gifts and then gave the kids a chance to start practicing. The kids received words of knowledge for people in the adult session, and they prayed for the adults who then received healing! One of the kids even prophesied to Euan a vision he had when he was 14 years old. It was exactly the same picture! The Holy Spirit's power is amazing, and it was so incredible to see the bold faith of the children that day, which resulted in multiple people being healed!

For me, the conference was eye-opening because I was raised in a much more conservative environment that did not teach on or encourage using the gifts of the Spirit. I realize that this is a touchy/sensitive topic for many believers in many denominations. However, this is not a topic I will skirt around. Jesus told His disciples to WAIT until the Holy Spirit arrived before they would be ready and equipped to go out into all the world to make disciples. Then the Holy Spirit showed up in power, and 11 disciples who had previously been so scared that they had run and hid suddenly had the courage and boldness to preach the gospel in such a way that thousands of people repented and came to believe in Jesus!

I don't think the Holy Spirit can be upon us, and, at the same time, we act totally normal and fit in with the world around us! I think the Holy Spirit brings Christians to a place of supernatural giftings that display to the world that Jesus is real. He is alive and active today, and He is attractive!

Ponder with Jesus

What about you? What experiences do you have with the gifts of the Spirit? Are they positive or negative? Or maybe non-existent? Are you carrying offense toward the gifts of the Spirit? Have you witnessed abuses of the gifts of the Spirit? Have you studied the gifts of the Spirit? Are you scared of them? Are you excited about them? Intrigued by them? Be honest with yourself and with God.

Repent of any offenses or fear you may have discovered. Then ask the Lord to reveal to you His heart regarding the gifts of the Spirit. Ask Him if there are any gifts He wants to give you today. Be open to receive—after all, they are good gifts given to us by our Good Father. If you don't know what to do with the gift you've been given, ask Jesus to tell you how to use it. And/or pray for a mentor to show you how to walk in it. God wants to empower us as His human partners to bring His Kingdom here and now and with power!

Chapter 14
Our #1 Calling in Life = Loving God

Jesus replied: "Love the Lord your God with all your heart and with all your soul and with all your mind." This is the first and greatest commandment.

~Matthew 22:37-38 NIV

While in Nepal, I spent a season studying The Song of Songs with Mike Bickle (International House Of Prayer, Kansas City). It opened my eyes to God's love in incredible ways. I highly recommend it to anyone seeking more intimacy with our Father. (They're free sermons with study notes online.)

Sometimes, we get so distracted by running, achieving, and striving to show God how much we love Him and want to serve Him. But really, He just wants us to love Him!

Imagine with me for a second ... a husband and wife have been super busy but finally have a weekend off work together. The husband is excited about some quality time together, anticipating a long walk on the beach and enjoying life-giving conversations. However, his wife is so busy trying to serve Him through cooking, cleaning, and getting their lives in order that she runs out of time to just be present with him. How devastating!

Similarly, I believe God wants us to just slow down and spend time loving and worshiping Him for who He is. Why is it so easy to prioritize serving over worshiping? We love to be busy for the Lord but often find it difficult to slow down enough to just soak in His presence and bow down to worship the King of Kings.

"Jesus said to him, *'You shall love the LORD your God with all your heart, with all your soul, and with all your mind.' This is the first and greatest commandment."* (Matthew 22:37-38 NIV)

In one of his sermons, Mike Bickle explains, "It is the first commandment because it is the first priority to God. It is not called the 'first option.' Loving God is an end in itself and is the highest lifestyle possible. It is the great commandment because it is always great in the impact it has on God's heart and our heart (and eventually others)."

For a few months during my time in Nepal, I lived alone and enjoyed living with Jesus as my only roommate. It was incredible to have a season of undistracted evenings with Jesus, and I truly fell more and more in love with Him through our uninterrupted time together. I would often start my evening with a worship song or two while I ate dinner, which helped focus my attention on Jesus and invited His presence to come. It's amazing how He can make

Himself known to us when we invite Him to come and then pay attention. Then we'd spend our evening together. I'd ask Him to highlight something He wanted to talk about or focus on. Then, I'd do whatever thought came to mind. Sometimes, that looked like listening to a sermon, reading the Bible, journal-praying (writing out my thoughts and prayers to Jesus—I stay much more focused writing than I do just thinking in my head), reading a Kingdom-focused book, or just worshiping Him and inviting Him to speak to my heart or show me pictures. There are a wide variety of spiritual disciplines and activities we can do to experience God in different ways. And He loves to show up when we're hungry to encounter Him. It's beautiful how loving God can look so different in each season of our lives. Loving God overflows to loving others, but only after we love Him with all our hearts, all our souls, and all our minds.

Ponder with Jesus

What about you? Would you classify your relationship with Jesus as intimate? Do you remember a past season of intimacy? Have you never even thought about it? I believe one of the easiest ways to fall in love with Jesus is to receive greater revelation of how He feels about us. Song of Songs can be interpreted in a couple of different ways, but one way is Jesus as the Bridegroom-King speaking to His bride—which is us. This is a passage I have read countless times because it reveals the Lord's heart toward us. He doesn't view us as weak and broken and useless. He says we are His beloved, His cherished bride. He, the Creator of heaven and earth, is undone by our love!?! Excuse me, wait, what did you say? Seriously? The Being that put the stars in their place is undone by my love? Mind blown.

Erika DeJonge

Stop. Take a deep breath. Focus your heart to receive from Jesus. Then, SLOWLY read this portion of Song of Songs 4. Maybe read it two or three times. What three truths stick out to you? What is Jesus saying to your heart? What does He call you? Who does He say you are?

Song of Songs 4:1-5 TPT
Listen, my dearest darling,
you are so beautiful—you are beauty itself to me!
Your eyes are
like gentle doves behind your veil.
What devotion I see each time I gaze upon you.
You are like a sacrifice ready to be offered.
When I look at you,
I see how you have taken my fruit and tasted my word.
Your life has become clean and pure,
like a lamb washed and newly shorn.
You now show grace and balance with truth on display.
Your lips are as lovely as Rahab's scarlet ribbon,
speaking mercy, speaking grace.
The words of your mouth are as refreshing as an oasis.
What pleasure you bring to me!
I see your blushing cheeks
opened like the halves of a pomegranate,
showing through your veil of tender meekness.
When I look at you,
I see your inner strength, so stately and strong.

You are as secure as David's fortress.
Your virtues and grace cause a thousand famous soldiers
to surrender to your beauty.
Your pure faith and love rest over your heart
as you nurture those who are yet infants.

How does your heart feel after basking in His love for you? Write a prayer of love and thanksgiving back to Jesus. Take time each day this week to reread this chapter. Let God's love pour over you and consume your heart. Invest some time in becoming intimate with your Lord, Savior, and Beloved Friend. I'm convinced there's nothing more important you could do with your time.

Chapter 15
Pursuing Justice

Vindicate the weak and fatherless; Do justice and maintain the rights of the afflicted and destitute. Rescue the weak and needy; Rescue them from the hand of the wicked.

~Psalm 82:3-4 AMP

I have found that once my heart is filled to overflowing with God's love for me, my focus turns upward, and He leads me to love Him back with all my heart, soul, and strength. Then my focus turns outward, and He calls me to love and serve the lost, the hurting, the broken, and the voiceless.

The following was written by one of the BFANepal interns, Rachel Bondi. During her month serving in Nepal, we visited the red-light district in Kathmandu. I feel that we experienced the following scene very similarly. I believe she captured the night perfectly, and I couldn't paint a more accurate picture if I tried.

Erika DeJonge

The Darkest Place

I walk in, and the air becomes unbearably heavy. Immediately, my heart drops to my toes, and my stomach is plagued with nausea. My ears are bombarded with painfully loud music. My eyes are attacked with flashing lights of every color. I begin to soak in the wildly devastating scene in front of me. It is a scene about which I have spent much time in thought and prayer but have never actually experienced. I think a part of me wondered if it would really be as bad as I'd imagined. It was worse.

I have walked into a dance club where women are being prostituted. There are women everywhere, clad in impossibly tiny dresses. Their faces are hidden behind what seems like infinite layers of makeup. They are sitting next to hungry men, allowing themselves to be pawed at. They are on the brightly lit stage, dancing for the delight of their onlookers. Most of them are 18-25 years old. Nothing in this life prepares you to walk into a place of such deep oppression. Every cell in my body wants to scream. The injustice is palpable! The idea that the bodies of my sisters are being sold for the vilely selfish pleasure of man is repulsive.

I sit down on a small couch with a few other missionaries. Soon, we are joined by a few of the women. We struggle with a significant language barrier and make valiant efforts to converse with them. We learn things about them, like their names, where they are from, and how long they have been working here. When they first sit down, they are smiling! But the longer we sit, the more the smiles fade, beginning to reveal the true emotion behind the carefully designed masks. In an attempt to offer a safe place to honestly discuss the reality of what is happening, I ask several of the women, "Do you like working here?" In four words that shatter my heart, one woman answers, "No one ever does."

In my two hours here, some women seemed open to talking to me. I have the honor of spending time with them, learning about their children, the things they like, and the things they dislike. Other women quickly turn away from me. The bar is full tonight, and they are eager for me to go away so they can earn money. Some are entirely opposed to the idea of vulnerability with a total stranger. And why shouldn't they be? Every stranger who walks into that bar has hands that exploit and a mouth that taunts. Why would I be any different?

When I walked out of that dance club, I was angry. I was angry with the Lord for graciously providing for me and seemingly neglecting the amazing women I had just met. Angry with the men I had seen, both the sellers and the clients. Angry with the world for failing these women so egregiously. Where is the justice? Who is fighting for them? I was filled with hopelessness. These women don't want to be working this way! But what are they supposed to do when the stomachs of their children grumble with the pains of starvation?

Everything is being taken from these women. Their bodies, the only thing they have to truly call their own, are no longer their own. They are so tragically devalued. They are taught that their pain, their devastation, and their voices don't matter. The hope they once had has been crushed by the greedy hands of man. These women deserve to know about their Champion, their Justice Seeker, their Victor. They deserve to know about their Advocate who gave up everything to know them—that night in the dance bar wrecked me. It challenged the things I thought I knew about the world. It broke my heart in ways I never knew it could be broken. It is undoubtedly the darkest place I have ever walked. But I am going back. They deserve to know of their Hero.

Open your mouth for the mute, For the rights of all the unfortunate. Open your mouth, judge righteously, And defend the rights of the afflicted and needy.

~Proverbs 31:8-9 NASB

Ponder with Jesus

Does this story break your heart? This undoubtedly breaks God's heart. This injustice is what brought me to Nepal in the first place. BFANepal provides employment to women rescued out of the sex industry so they are able to provide for themselves and their families. Without good employment options, many women rescued out of the sex industry end up returning due to a lack of alternate options.

But this is just one of many injustices in the world. There are countless situations in your backyard and around the world that break God's heart every day—and He's continuously calling His human partners to do something about it. He gave the Holy Spirit to empower His children, His image bearers, to do His work—To bring His Kingdom on earth as it is in heaven.

Is there a particular injustice that rips your heart into pieces? Is there anything you're fighting for? Is there a group of people that you have a burden for? If so, ask the Lord what you need to do to fight for them. Then stop, look, and listen—and then, of course, obey.

If not, start by praying a simple yet powerful prayer. "Lord, please break my heart for what breaks Yours." It's a prayer He loves to answer. Then pay attention! What stories on the news break your heart? Is it the poor and homeless population? The refugees? Victims of domestic violence? The killing of unborn children? The breakdown of the family in America? What injustice is the Lord calling you to engage with?

Ask the Lord to break your heart for what breaks His. Then, pay attention. Stop, look, and listen. As He reveals it to you, ask Him, "What's the first step You want me to take to engage with this injustice." Then go do it.

Chapter 16
Complete Dependence

Think about the lilies. They grow and become beautiful, not because they work hard or strive to clothe themselves. Yet not even Solomon, wearing his kingly garments of splendor, could be compared to a field of lilies.

~Luke 12:27 TPT

About a year into my time in Nepal, I came home for a furlough. While spending a weekend exploring God's country (aka Northern Michigan) with friends, one of my friends asked, "What about life in Nepal do you miss the most?" It didn't take long for me to realize that the hardest part about being here instead of there is how drastically my relationship with God is affected. I would like to tell you that everything I learned and experienced in Nepal translates easily to my walk with God in Michigan. Unfortunately, it does not.

In America, it's easy to have this false sense of independence. If my car breaks down, I have countless family members and friends to call for help. If I get in a car accident, there is car insurance, health insurance, and ICU's to fix my injuries, etc. Conversely, in Nepal, if my motorcycle doesn't start, I'm far more likely to assess my resources and immediately turn to my Heavenly Father for help! I would pray each day on my motorcycle for God's protection. Here, it's easy to hop in the car without even thinking about safety. There, it's much "easier" to live in complete dependence and awareness of God's provision in my life. It is truly humbling to realize how easily I slip from complete dependence on God to this independent, "self-sufficient" living.

The day after this question was posed to me, I was practicing riding my brother's motorcycle for the motorcycle endorsement skills test (so I could more confidently drive my motorcycle in Nepal) when we noticed that the taillight was not working. Unfortunately, they will not allow you to test for your endorsement unless the bike is in complete working order with ALL the lights working appropriately. It was late Sunday night, so we agreed to address it the following day when we had more energy and parts stores would be open.

My exam was in less than 24 hours, making it imperative that the motorcycle be fixed immediately. It was Monday night, and I was heading over to my brother Luke's house to attempt to fix the tail light. As he was giving me instructions over the phone, the conversation with my friends came to mind, and I told Luke that I was just going to pray for Jesus to fix the motorcycle so I wouldn't have to worry about it. After all, He is a Good Father who loves to take care of His children. We agreed that if I prayed and the light was still broken, I would call him back for further instructions.

So, I arrived at Luke's house and immediately started unscrewing the tail light—yup, that's how quickly I reverted back to independence mode. Less than five minutes after my discussion with Luke about praying for God to intervene, I was back to attempting to fix things on my own. While I was unscrewing the first screw, I was reminded of my desire to depend on God. I immediately stopped and prayed.

I wish I could tell you it was some eloquent prayer that was full of faith and confidence, but it sounded more like, "Hey God, I can't believe how quickly I forget to depend on You. I'm so sorry. I'm not going to lie; I'm exhausted, and I just don't feel like dealing with this. I know You can fix this in an instant, no problem. Would You mind just fixing this so I can go hang out with Mom and the kids before dinner?" I set the screwdriver down and grabbed the keys instead. And you know what? When I turned the key, the tail light was as good as new!!! I was ecstatic, relieved, and humbled.

How often do we leave God out of the picture because we can just take care of it ourselves? Sometimes, I feel like a two-year-old who's determined to dress herself—yeah, she can make it happen—but if she'd just let her parents help, it'd be a much easier process with a much prettier result. God cares deeply about the details of our lives. He cares about the tail lights in our lives. He loves to give us good gifts! And He cares about doing life with us.

Ponder with Jesus

What about you? What parts of your life do you forget to invite Him into because you're just so stubbornly independent? Pray with me, "Father God, I surrender my independence to You and pray You'll open my eyes to see how You're intricately involved in my life. Please show me. Is there an area of my life where I am too fiercely independent? Thanks for doing life with me and for never leaving me to figure it out on my own."

Then, stop, look, and listen. Is there an area of your life God wants you to surrender control and trust Him to work things out for you? Go on a journey with Him and ask Him to help you surrender completely. Ask for tangible steps of what that might look like. Then do it!

Chapter 17
Surrender, Sacrifice, and Suffering

Saying, "Father, if you are willing, remove this cup from me. Nevertheless, not my will, but yours, be done."

~Luke 22:42 ESV

It was New Year's night, and I was driving away from saying goodbye to my siblings, two nieces, and nephew for the last time. I didn't know the next time I'd be back in Michigan and could only imagine how big those beloved kids would be by the time I returned. Needless to say—I was a wreck. As I drove across town, I just wept. I remember pulling up to a stoplight and just sobbing. At that moment, I cried out to God, "Why does it have to hurt so much?" Instantly, I felt His immense peace and His indescribable comfort come over me with the thought, *"I've been there. I know it hurts, and I am with you."*

Jesus has been through more pain and turmoil than I can imagine. I cannot even comprehend the excruciating suffering He endured the night He was killed—the day He was abandoned by His closest friends. At the same time, He was tortured, beaten, and eventually murdered. My God is not some distant and foreign god demanding sacrifice without firsthand experience of true suffering. There is immense comfort in knowing that my God understands true surrender, true sacrifice, true suffering, and true love. He understands that goodbyes are hard. I serve a God who has lived, loved, and wept. My Jesus understands painful obedience, and in the end, He said, *"Not My will, but Yours be done"* (Luke 22:42 NASB). And therefore, with His help, I said the same; "Not my will, but Yours be done." And I hopped back on that plane to Nepal.

Ponder with Jesus

Will you say the same? "Not my will, but Yours be done." Say it with me. "Not my will, but Yours be done." Ask the Lord to reveal to you any times you've selfishly said, "Not Your will, but mine be done." Repent and confess anything that comes to mind. Then ask the Lord, "Are there any situations in my life right now where I am fighting for my will to be done over Yours?" Then stop, look, and listen. Repent means to turn and go in a different direction. In any situation the Lord brings to mind, repent. Surrender your will, sacrifice your desires, and submit to His lordship in your life. It's the best choice you'll ever make—no matter how much it hurts.

Chapter 18
The God of Miracles

Very truly I tell you, whoever believes in me will do the works I have been doing, and they will do even greater things than these, because I am going to the Father.

~John 14:12 NIV

Glenda (BFANepal Executive Director), Liv (new BFANepal designer and roommate), and I helped host the Open Heaven Conference again in my second year in Nepal. That's the prophetic conference with speakers from Australia, Finland, the U.K., and America. The goal of the conference was to encourage the missionaries, leaders, and teachers of Nepal and India. The worship and teaching were all in English (a treat for us) and directed toward mature believers. There was also a lot of worship and ministry time, which was so encouraging and refreshing.

One thing we did at the conference was lead people in an

experience called an encounter. It's a time when we use our God-given imaginations to encounter heaven. Basically, we ask God to reveal things to us through a time of imagining with Him. On this particular encounter in India, we went into the storehouse of heaven and were told that God wanted to give us something. I asked God what He wanted to give me, and He said, *"The gift of healing—physical, emotional, and spiritual healing."* Someone once prophesied over me that God wanted to use me to bring healing, so this wasn't an entirely new idea, but one I definitely wasn't expecting to hear. I asked God how to use the gift of healing and felt Him say, *"Just start practicing it; start walking it out."* I immediately thought of my experience just two days prior on a flight to India, where I felt prompted to pray for a nonbeliever but didn't ask to pray for him out of fear of him not being healed. So, I quickly turned back to God and said, "Can I also have a gift of faith? Because just two days ago, I failed miserably." I felt Him chuckle and say, *"Of course, you're in the storehouse of heaven! Take a gift of faith as well!"* And so, I did.

Not five minutes later, I met a girl named Miracle. She was maybe eight years old. As she shared her name, I was reminded how our words and names have power and significance. I said, "Miracle! It's so great to meet you. I just know that you are going to see miracles happen in your life!" She replied, "I already do! I see angels." I got so excited as I'd been praying for God to open my eyes to see more of the supernatural, so I asked her to pray for me—so I could see angels, too. She readily agreed, put her little hand on my shoulder, and prayed, "Dear God, please let Erika see angels like I do. Amen."

As I looked up, I saw another teammate, Gracie—who happened to have one pinkie that was shorter than the other because of a childhood accident. I said, "Hey, Miracle, let's ask God for another miracle—do you want to pray for my friend's finger to grow out?" She looked surprised yet filled with excitement. Glenda (who was nearby) and I both prayed for Gracie's finger to grow out. I peeked to see if it had grown—it hadn't. Then Miracle prayed, "Dear God, please heal Gracie's finger so it's like the other one. Amen." We opened our eyes and, what do you know? Her pinkies were the exact same length!!! It was in that moment that God revealed to me the power of having faith like a child.

You see, while Glenda and I were praying, I was so worried that we would pray and God wouldn't heal her finger, and Miracle would forever lose faith in the God of miracles. Yet God was using the experience not only to increase Miracle's faith but mine as well. I suppose it was in that moment that God granted me the gift of faith I had asked for just five minutes earlier. In the following hours, God used that gift of faith to help me encourage and minister to those at the conference. It was such an exciting time of stepping out in faith and watching God show up and speak clearly. I cannot begin to share all of the stories, but the Holy Spirit moved powerfully—in my life and in the lives of those around us. It was a wildly exciting time that will not soon be forgotten.

Ponder with Jesus

What about you? Do you believe in miracles? Or have you been taught that miracles and gifts of the spirit ended with the 12 disciples? Do you believe God wants to show up in your life and provide for you in supernatural ways? Or do you have God in a box—forced to work within the framework of what you know and expect of Him? I was not raised in an environment that fostered faith for miracles, but after receiving miraculous healing for myself and witnessing miraculous healing for others, I can promise you—God is so much bigger than we know Him to be! Do you need a miracle in your life? Are you skeptical? Ask the Lord what He thinks of miracles. Then stop, look, and listen to His response.

Close your eyes and think of your biggest struggle or obstacle in your life right now. Then, with your eyes closed, ask the Lord what He wants to do about it. Then stop, look, and listen. He has supernatural solutions to all of our earthly problems. Close with a prayer asking God to accomplish His will on earth as it is in heaven—God has won. Nothing is impossible for God. You are a child of God! May His will be done in your life.

This is where the adventures kick in—asking the Lord to move mountains and do miracles. Often, He asks for us to participate with Him, to pray for the miracle to happen, or to declare that it is happening. He loves to partner with us, and it can be an absolutely terrifying and exhilarating ride! Will you step out in faith for God to show up in miraculous ways? By now, you know what I think—I think He's worth it—every time!

Chapter 19
Freedom from Unforgiveness

Do not judge, and you will not be judged. Do not condemn, and you will not be condemned. Forgive, and you will be forgiven.

~Luke 6:37 NIV

Valentine's Day in Nepal is always a joyous occasion at BFANepal, but this year, in particular, it was brought to a whole new level! We were honored to have Heidi Baker visit us and share Christ's love with us all the way from Mozambique. Heidi and her husband, Rolland, are the Founding Directors of Iris Global, which now has 15 bases worldwide and has planted thousands of churches. Heidi travels the world and often speaks to thousands of people at large gatherings, but we were honored to have her visit us and spend intimate time with just our little BFANepal family.

The women were impressed that, although she is famous and

travels the world speaking to large crowds, she came and sat right down on the ground and started asking them about their lives and their families. She didn't march in as someone important to quickly speak and leave. She wanted to sit and truly be present with them.

Heidi connected to our women as one "mama" to other "mamas". Regardless of color, culture, language, age, location, or circumstance, every mama's heart is to love and protect her children at any cost. Heidi shared about the healing power of grace and forgiveness and how when we forgive—both ourselves and others—we find freedom from the burden of harboring unforgiveness and bitterness.

She spent time praying for our women and encouraging them. The Holy Spirit showed up in amazing ways, and many women shared they had never had such a powerful encounter with the Holy Spirit before! For some of the women that looked like weeping and allowing God to come in and heal past hurts as He helped them forgive. For others, it looked like dancing, laughing, and immense joy. Many of the women felt her story and message were specifically shared for them. I personally felt totally seen and loved by God. As Heidi hugged me, she told me that God sees my life as the oil of sacrifice being poured out on His feet—that my entire life is oil being poured out, and God is so blessed by my life of love, intimacy, and sacrifice. Of course, Heidi didn't know me or my story, but she hears clearly from the Lord, so I trust His eyes are on me, and He sees my life of love poured out as a living sacrifice to Him. I felt so loved and encouraged. As with every great BFANepal family gathering, a dance party broke out, and we ended our time together with singing, dancing, and photos.

Ponder with Jesus

What about you? Are you harboring any unforgiveness or bitterness? I know we've talked about it before, but I feel very strongly that the Lord wants His children to walk in complete and absolute freedom! You cannot walk in peace, joy, and freedom while also harboring bitterness, offense, and unforgiveness. Is your slate really clean? Be honest with yourself before the Lord. Did you forgive everyone except that one unforgivable offense? Here's your second chance. Forgive them now. Choose the abundant life of freedom that is available thanks to Christ's shed blood on the cross!

If you just can't forgive them, pray the prayer, "Lord, please make me willing to be made willing to forgive this person." Then, ask the Lord to give you a picture of how He sees that person. Stop, look, and listen. I expect God to show you a picture that helps you have compassion. When you have a heart of compassion for someone, it's instantly easier to forgive. Forgiveness doesn't mean that what they did was right. It just releases you from carrying the hatred and puts it in God's hands to vindicate. Trust the Lord's leadership in your life. He wants what is best for you, and He says to forgive seventy times seven!

Chapter 20
Bringing Shalom to Chaos

Hear, O Israel: The Lord our God, the Lord is one! You shall love the Lord your God with all your heart, with all your soul, and with all your strength.

~Deuteronomy 6:4-5 NIV

While living in Nepal, I took two weeks away to go on a study tour through Israel with a friend. Studying my way through Israel forever impacted my walk with Jesus. I cannot express strongly enough how incredible the trip was. The Bible totally came alive! There are so many fabulous parallels between the Old and New Testaments that I have always glossed over in ignorance. Throughout our two-week trip, we journeyed through a narrative that started in the Old Testament in the wilderness. We followed one continuous story and, therefore, one continuous mission from Genesis to Jesus and beyond (through us, His human partners).

To put it simply, God chose Israel to be His human partners, and they screwed it up. But God is faithful and chose to use the Israelites despite their adulterous nature. Jesus simply came to show us how to walk the righteous path that He called us (Israel) to so long ago. His mission has always been for us to bring shalom (fullness/wholeness/peace) to the chaos of the world. Wherever there is chaos, we need to bring shalom to put our God on display and to reflect His perfect love to the world.

Of course, we saw the major sites and engaged in this story from day one to ten as we covered the desert/wilderness in the south and the beautiful Sea of Galilee in the north. Finally, we made it to Jerusalem. It was just absolutely phenomenal!

But as I returned to Nepal, I felt the weight of what it takes to stay on the righteous path. Bringing shalom to chaos is not easy and is often quite costly—if Jesus was the perfect example of what walking the righteous path looks like—it looks to me like it costs absolutely everything.

And so, I returned to Nepal wondering how on earth am I going to put all of this into practice? It was much easier to walk around the beautiful Holy Land and talk about all the people who have gone before us and how they failed or did it well. It was much easier to go back to our air-conditioned hotel rooms with luxuriously high-pressured, clean-water showers (in stark contrast to the brown-water showers we enjoyed in Nepal). It was a bit of a reality check walking back into the chaos of Kathmandu, knowing that this was the place where God had called me to engage the chaos. I was humbled that God would choose to use me, and then I was really lost on where to start.

As I descended into the Kathmandu Valley, I again clung to the promise that God is faithful. He is faithful. And He would continue to lead and guide me. He would continue to enable me to bring shalom to the chaos of this world. I just needed to remain in a place of complete surrender and complete dependence on Him.

Ponder with Jesus

What about you? Are you bringing shalom to the chaos around you? Or are you easily weighed down by the chaos surrounding you? Have you joined the mission? Are you engaging with the chaos and bringing shalom?

Think about the people around you. Are there any situations that feel chaotic? Maybe it's a friend, family member, or coworker who is experiencing loss, pain, or turmoil. Ask the Lord to bring to mind one tangible thing you could do to bring shalom to their chaos. Then stop, look, and listen—and then do it.

CHAPTER 21
THE WEDDING AT SINAI

You shall have no other gods before me.

~Exodus 20:3 NIV

I want to share one of the countless pictures I learned to see more clearly during my time in Israel, studying with David Mosterd while on a KINGdom Story Project Biblical Study Tour. While in Israel, I discovered we miss out on so much of the Bible when we disconnect ourselves from our Jewish roots.

I want to tell you about the Jewish people's perspective on Exodus 19 (the story of the Israelites leaving Egypt and meeting God at Sinai). It comes from rabbinic thought coming from Hallel, who starts to read this text and puts it together in a particular way alongside two other scriptures. He predates Jesus by about 100 years.

Jeremiah 2:1-4 God is saying to the prophet Jeremiah, *"Remember* when you were young, right when I took you out of slavery? Out of bondage? Remember how I led you into the wilderness—like a bride!"

Isaiah 54:5-6 (NIV)

For your Maker is your husband—

the Lord Almighty is his name—

the Holy One of Israel is your Redeemer;

he is called the God of all the earth.

The Lord will call you back

as if you were a wife deserted and distressed in spirit—

a wife who married young,

only to be rejected," says your God.

Sinai is a wedding! God says, *"I will take you out of slavery. I will take away your slave nature. I will give you a new identity because I redeemed you. I'll pay the price. I will take you to myself, to know you, so that you are known. And you will be my bride and I will be your husband."*

Let's start by reviewing the steps of a traditional Jewish marriage:

1. It starts with a **courtship** and in that process, you'd get to know each other. Sometimes quickly, sometimes it would take longer, but you would take time to get to know your future spouse.

2. Then, there was an exchange of **possessions**. A bride price or something exchanged that symbolized the importance

of this relationship. Something important and valuable is happening here, so there's an exchange of possessions to give us a physical and material representation of that process.

3. **Consecration** is the step where the bride would wash on the day of her wedding to consecrate and purify herself.

4. Then the couple would come and stand under a **covering** to show that they will stand under the covering of God as He blesses and anoints the relationship.

5. There were **vows** exchanged. There were words exchanged to say that they committed themselves fully, wholly, and completely to each other.

So, this is how, in the Jewish tradition, a relationship moves from two people who are separate to becoming one.

Let's look at God bringing Israel out of Egypt in Genesis 19-20 through this lens.

1. Is there a **courtship** between God and His people? God says, "*I will come down, release you from bondage, and redeem you.*" From the day of Passover, until they arrive at Sinai, they have 40 days to get to know each other.

2. Is there an exchange of **possessions**? Let's come back to this one later.

3. Is there a **consecration**? Yes, God says, "*Moses, go down and tell the people to consecrate themselves before I meet with them.*" (Exodus 19:10)

4. Is there a **covering**? Exodus 19:17 says, "A dark and deep

cloud has come down to cover the mountain" (TPT).

5. Are there **vows**? Listen to Exodus 20, the 10 commandments as vows:

"I will be your husband. I will take away your slave nature. I will redeem you! I don't want any other girlfriends—no other spouses! I don't even want pictures of them—just you and me. So, get rid of your old boyfriends, and get rid of their pictures, too. I want a date night. I want just one day a week for me and you—don't let the other stuff of this world get in the way. I'm your husband and I want to be with you!"

These aren't dos and don'ts. They're wedding vows! When a husband and wife make vows, they don't think of them as a list of dos and don'ts. They just love each other. They want to continue to get to know each other more and more. God brings His people to a mountain and says, *"Will you marry me?"*

If we're going to be a kingdom of priests, we have to take our vows seriously! We can't empty his name—we have to fill it up! We have to be patient. We have to trust him—that He has our best intentions in mind. He'll do anything necessary to redeem us and to bring us home so that we might be His human partners.

Let's go back to #2. The exchange of valuable **possessions**. What was God giving the Israelites? Himself. Is there anything more valuable on earth? Not a thing. What valuables did the Israelites have, and what did they choose to do with them? In Exodus 25, God asks for an offering of gold, silver, bronze, linen, wood, and oil, etc. Then, He tells Moses to have them make a sanctuary so He can dwell among them. (This will eventually be where they consummate the marriage).

But what did they give their gold jewelry to instead? In chapter 32, they give all of their jewelry to Aaron to make them a golden calf to worship.

During their very wedding week, they were sleeping around with other girlfriends!?!

As I heard this, my heart just broke! As I envisioned a husband the morning of his wedding chucking a wedding ring across the room and shouting, "It's off—the wedding is off! You screwed it up, you foolish woman! I was ready to redeem you, to set you free. I was ready to welcome you into my home and my family—provide for your every need and protect you. I was ready to love and pursue you perfectly from now until forever! But NO! You just had to screw it up! The wedding is off!"

But God quickly whispered, *"No, no. The wedding is still on!"*

What??? What kind of love is this? What kind of husband marries a woman who was sleeping around just last night? How can You choose to love and forgive when I so quickly turn back to my old ways, my old lovers, my old self? How absolutely reckless to continue to choose love when I continue to hurt You over and over and over again? Do You know how often I'll screw up? Do You know how often You'll have to fight for me and continue to pursue me as I sleep around with old lovers? Do You have any idea how stubborn and rebellious I am?

And God says, "Yes. *I know. I still say, 'I do.'"*

But then He asks, "Will you?"

Erika DeJonge

Ponder with Jesus

So, will you? Will you marry Him? Will you say "I do?" It might mean He takes you into the desert. It might mean He asks you to climb a mountain you never intended to climb. Will you say "I do"? Or will you choose the idols of this world—busyness, material things, hobbies, even family, friends, jobs—good things put in the wrong place of importance? Will you commit to this covenant love? Or are you going to pursue other lovers?

Sit quietly with the Lord and repent of anything that has received more attention or affection than it should have. Recommit to putting Him first and foremost in your life. Recommit to your First Love.

Chapter 22
A Call to Radical Hospitality

When a stranger sojourns with you in your land, you shall not do him wrong. You shall treat the stranger who sojourns with you as the native among you, and you shall love him as yourself, for you were strangers in the land of Egypt: I am the Lord your God.

~Leviticus 19: 33-34 ESV

During my time in Israel, we learned how God called Israel to stand out and look different. God commanded Israel to be laid out in such a way that foreigners and travelers passing through could stop at the city gate and be replenished. He commanded them to build their cities with the storehouses right by the city gates. The average city in those days was set up for protection—keeping the storehouses far from the city gates to keep their supplies safe and protected. But not Israel. The God of Israel would protect them and fight their battles, but Israel was supposed to feed the weary traveler, take care of the widows, and replenish the foreigners passing through while trusting God to take care of their needs. You see, God was setting up Israel to invite the foreigners in and bless them. God has always sought to save the lost. He didn't choose Israel as His chosen people just for their sake. No! He wanted to bless the nations through them. He wanted them to display His goodness and His character to everyone who passed by—inviting them into His Kingdom.

Before leaving for Israel, my friend and roommate Liv gave me a prophetic word. She said, "I feel like God is saying, *'He's going to start speaking into the next season while keeping your heart planted in this one.'*" This word was readily received as I honestly still couldn't picture leaving Nepal to move back to America. I knew when God called me to Nepal that He called me for three years. The funny thing is, when He told me that, I didn't have faith for it, so I committed for "one to probably three years." Then, once I got to Nepal, I felt so fulfilled and satisfied I was finally living a purpose-filled life. It's like I was finally living the life I had talked about for so many years. What does it look like to live differently? To live for Jesus? This is it! So when people asked how long I'd stay in Nepal, I'd tell them, "At least three years." But as I prepared to go to Israel, I still couldn't picture how I would ever move back to America while continuing to live a purpose-filled life.

So, as I walked through Israel, learning more about my Jewish roots, I felt God highlighting to me radical hospitality as part of my call back to America. The Israelites were called to live in such a way that they put serving over protecting. I, too, am called to live in such a way that my home is for serving, not protecting. And the Lord brought to mind the different types of poverty in the world. I was living in a third-world country. Physical poverty was all around me. But when I thought of America, a different kind of poverty became evident—relational poverty. In America, everyone lives in their own home with their own car, their own washing machine, lawn mower, and snow blower. People tend not to need their neighbors because they are already self-sufficient. In Nepal, you'd see neighbors sitting around drinking tea and living in community day and night. There were community bathrooms, community laundry areas, traveling together by foot or bus, etc. In America, we're so self-sufficient and independent that we lose out on relationships. There are unprecedented amounts of anxiety, depression, and suicide in America right now. Why? I believe this is because people are more isolated and further from living in community than ever before. I believe strongly that we were designed to do life together and with Jesus at the center. Only then can we walk in freedom, peace, and joy.

We as Christians are called to live in such a way that invites the stranger in, feeds the hungry, clothes the orphan, and blesses the foreigner—all to bring God glory and invite others into relationship with Him. It was through this revelation that I began to feel the Lord call me back to America. I realized I wanted my home to be a place that displays radical hospitality to a land that is crying out for true community and true relationships.

Ponder with Jesus

What about you? Have you ever considered hospitality a way to display God's goodness to your neighbors? How could your home become a safe place for the weary traveler, the refugee, the foreigner, or the oppressed? Have you considered engaging your neighbors in conversation as a way to bring God's Kingdom to your neighborhood? What if transforming your neighborhood could start with you? Ask the Lord if your home is set up to serve Him and bring glory to His name or if anything needs to change. Ask the Lord, "What's one tangible step I can take this month to make my home a place of refuge for those who need it most?" Then stop, look, and listen. Whatever you hear, see, or sense, make it happen!

Chapter 23
Iron-Sharpens-Iron Community

And let us consider how we may spur one another on toward love and good deeds, not giving up meeting together, as some are in the habit of doing, but encouraging one another—and all the more as you see the Day approaching.

~Hebrews 10:24-25 NIV

For over six weeks after arriving back in Kathmandu from Israel, I struggled off and on with feeling overwhelmed by just how much chaos there was in Nepal. I knew I was simply called to bring God's shalom to the people around me, but sometimes, the brokenness and hopelessness there clouded my vision. On top of that, the stunning and pure beauty of Israel made the lack of beauty in Kathmandu Valley feel all the more stifling.

Therefore, Liv (BFA designer, friend, and roommate) and I went to visit our friend who managed the BFANepal remote branch office in a village five hours away. It was a rainy, dreary weekend, but it was oh-so refreshing to my soul to be able to meet with Jesus in His beautiful creation with a few other like-minded believers. It turned out to be exactly what I needed!

I've realized I wouldn't have made it through my three years in Nepal without the laid-down lovers of Jesus (people who have willingly laid down everything to love and worship their King) I encountered during my time there. Each and every missionary friend I found had made the costly choice to leave the comfort and abundance of the Western world and had left behind family and friends to obey the One who is worth it all. I thoroughly enjoyed multiple Bible studies and fellowships with an assortment of people from a variety of countries and truly grew in my faith in ways I never thought possible. I was continually learning new things about God and how earnestly He longs to be in relationship with each of His children. We're not called to do it alone. And I could not be more thankful that God put me in community to work together to bring shalom to the chaos of Kathmandu.

Ponder with Jesus

What about you? Are you immersed in a Christ-centered community? Do you have iron-sharpening-iron friendships? Or are you trying to live out your faith on your own? Are you surrounding yourself with people who are pursuing Jesus at all costs? Or are you happy hanging around people who leave you comfortable where you are? God wants to GROW in relationship with us—that means there will be mountains and valleys. There will be dry seasons and seasons of abundance, but He doesn't want any of our seasons to be attempted alone. What steps can you take to surround yourself with laid-down lovers of Jesus? Are you involved in a Bible study? Are you actively involved in a local church? Are you engaging your friends in spiritual conversations?

Ask the Lord to speak into your situation. "Jesus, what's one step I can take to further immerse myself in Christian community?" Then stop, look, and listen. And, of course, do what He says.

Chapter 24
Learning to Worship

And Samuel said, "Has the Lord as great delight in burnt offerings and sacrifices, as in obeying the voice of the Lord? Behold, to obey is better than sacrifice, and to listen than the fat of rams."

~1 Samuel 15:22 ESV

My definition of worship grew and expanded dramatically throughout my time in Nepal. Before a new year began, I asked God what He wanted to teach me in the coming year. I felt Him say, *"The coming year will be a year of learning to be an extravagant worshiper."* I had no idea the depth of that statement. I think I pictured learning to dance during praise and worship. It turns out there's so much more!

For a few weeks, I felt like God was bombarding me with different perspectives on worship. In Bible study, we were studying the life of David—which, of course, talks about David's heart of worship unto the Lord. I was also reading three other books which all touched on worship in the same two weeks.

Through it all, I learned that extravagant worship is all about a surrendered life full of obedience. Yes, the Lord wants our praise and our worship, but more than anything, He wants to be intricately involved in every detail of our lives, and He is honored and worshiped when we surrender completely to Him. Psalm 37:23 says, "The steps of the godly are directed by the Lord. He delights in every detail of their lives" (NLT).

According to *The Purpose Driven Life* by Rick Warren, "Learning to love God and be loved by Him should be the greatest objective of your life." And also, "When you feel abandoned by God, yet continue to trust Him in spite of your feelings, you worship Him in the deepest way." The heart of worship isn't dancing. It's surrender—to be an extravagant worshiper, I need to be dramatically surrendered to God!

Brother Lawrence, in *Practicing the Presence of God* says, "The goal of the spiritual life is to become the most perfect worshipers of God that we can possibly be, in this life and throughout all eternity." And I could really relate to Gene Edwards, who says in *100 Days in the Secret Place*, "To want to serve God in some conditions, but not others, is to serve Him in your own way. But to put no limits on your submission to God is truly dying to yourself. This is how to worship God!" It just seemed to me that God was highlighting over and over again His desire for surrender and obedience as the ultimate act of worship.

That summer required me to come back to a place of true surrender.

The reality of Nepal had felt more difficult, and my perspective needed to be renewed. Work felt less rewarding, life felt harder, and home felt extra far away. So, as I was reminded that truly extravagant worship means truly extravagant surrender, I had also been learning to depend on God's strength when I felt too weak or inadequate for the task at hand. Thankfully, God promised to guide me and to always be enough, so I could continue to choose to surrender everything I am and everything I do to the One Who is worthy of all my worship!

Ponder with Jesus

So, how's your worship these days? Are you worshiping God with all that you are and all that you have? Or are you holding back? Is your heart in a place of complete surrender? Because we don't get to worship God on our terms, it's all or nothing. Is He Lord of your entire life? Is He the pilot or co-pilot? Are you calling the shots and asking Him to bless your path? Or are you listening and obeying the One Who made you? Are you completely surrendered to His will for your life? That is true and extravagant worship.

Spend some quiet time before the Lord and ask Him to reveal to you any areas of your life that you're withholding from His Lordship. Commit to yourself and to the Lord to live a life of complete surrender from this day forward.

A wise friend once told me marriage was harder yet better than being single. I feel like it's the same with God. There are many days that living a worldly life looks easier, but even when life with Jesus can feel harder at times, I have to believe it's always better!

Chapter 25
Sabbath Rest

Remember the Sabbath day by keeping it holy. Six days you shall labor and do all your work, but the seventh day is a Sabbath to the Lord your God. On it you shall not do any work, neither you, nor your son or daughter, nor your male or female servant, nor your animals, nor any foreigner residing in your towns. For in six days the Lord made the heavens and the earth, the sea, and all that is in them, but he rested on the seventh day. Therefore the Lord blessed the Sabbath day and made it holy.

~Exodus 20:8-11 NIV

One lesson I learned to take seriously during my time in Nepal was Sabbath rest. Nepal felt a bit like a pressure cooker. Life was harder. The comforts of home were missing. We were operating in a foreign language and driving on the left side of the road in a ridiculously chaotic, dirty, and loud city. One could say that life felt more wearisome in Nepal than in America. So, when I skipped my Sabbath, the consequences were more noticeable. I think this is another area where it's easy to go soft and ignore scripture because we're too busy, have different priorities, and find it inconvenient to set aside 24 hours a week for our Lord. This simply should not be.

While in Nepal, the Lord brought me to a sermon about rest by Michael Miller at the Upper Room. The sermon really convicted me and reminded me why Sabbath rest is so incredibly important. The following points come almost entirely from this sermon. I highly recommend listening to it in its entirety.

Is rest the first thing that comes to mind when you picture holiness? Yeah, me neither. But God's ways are higher than ours. Sabbath rest was the very first thing in the whole Bible to be declared holy! And He declares that busyness and burning yourself out and pushing yourself to the end of your rope actually isn't holy. Resting in the finished work of Jesus is holy. Isn't our Father just so good?

In Genesis 2, day seven of creation comes around, and the Lord's work of creating the entire world is completed. It was done, He was finished. Then He rested. He did not rest from His work because He was tired or because He was modeling for us how to live. The Lord rested from His work because it was complete and done. Like a painter would rest after painting the greatest masterpiece, he would cease to work because there was nothing else to do. This is the type of rest God was taking on day seven. The Sabbath rest reality was supposed to be present for the rest of creation!

On day seven, Adam awakes for his first day as a human and is immersed in the rest and finished work of God. Adam was to live from that place perpetually. Work would be purposeful and include co-laboring with God. Adam would bear fruit, but it would always be born out of a place of rest. I think we've lost some of this beautiful revelation, and it's time to return to honoring the Sabbath and keeping it holy.

The Sabbath is also a witness to ourselves and to the world that we trust God enough to give Him one day a week. Miller, in the sermon, goes on to share that Chick-fil-A is a business that honors the Sabbath and keeps it holy. You cannot enjoy a scrumptious Chick-fil-A sandwich after church on Sunday because they are closed! McDonalds, however, is wide open and available every day of the week. Would you believe that, on average, per franchise, Chick-fil-A actually brings in more sales than McDonalds even though McDonalds is open one more day per week? That doesn't make any sense! But God can do more in six days than we can do in seven. The Sabbath is a witness to you, to me, and to the rest of the world that our God is powerful and He is fighting for us, and He calls us to be still and rest in His finished work.

You probably haven't thought about stealing from the grocery store this week or cheating on your spouse this week. So why do we think it's okay to totally ignore one of the top ten commandments from our God? It just doesn't make sense. If He is truly our First Love, if we're really going to marry Him and surrender our lives to His Lordship, it's time we say "I do" and stick to our wedding vows. It's time we give God our date night back. He's so worth it!

Ponder with Jesus

What about you? Do you take a day of rest each week? Or do you think you can run faster and run harder and get further ahead on your own rather than letting the Lord rejuvenate you each week?

Are there any lies you're believing that are getting in the way of honoring the Sabbath and keeping it holy? Have you gotten caught up in American culture and the never-ending rat race that makes Sabbathing especially hard? It sure is easy to do. Is it possible that Sabbathing in our current culture could make your witness even more powerful? Do you believe God can do more with six days a week than you can do with seven? Ask the Lord if He will show Himself faithful to you if you love Him sacrificially by honoring the Sabbath. Journal His response. What does He want to do for you? What is He promising you?

This chapter may feel off-topic, but doesn't disregarding one of the ten commandments sound like a sin? And is it possible that habitual sin could quickly impede our ability to hear from and commune with God? I don't know about you, but I don't want ANYTHING standing between me and my Father. Are you settling for less and allowing sin to get in the way of hearing His voice? Could a lack of Sabbathing be standing between you and intimacy with Jesus? Are you going to tolerate that? Or are you willing to do something about it? If you're feeling convicted, repent of breaking your wedding vows. But remember how quick the Lord is to forgive and continue to commit to you. He still wants to marry you and still wants to talk to you!

So, stop and ask the Lord, "Jesus, what steps do I need to take to honor the Sabbath and keep it holy?" What does rest look like for me in this season? Then stop, look, and listen. Then, of course, commit to the righteous path and work to honor your commitment to the Lord your God. Just like Chick-fil-A, you won't regret it!

Chapter 26
Celebrating God's Faithfulness

Let your roots grow down into him, and let your lives be built on him. Then your faith will grow strong in the truth you were taught, and you will overflow with thankfulness.

~Colossians 2:6-7 NLT

For BFANepal's 10-year birthday party, we got all dressed up in beautiful, colorful saris (Nepali traditional dress which is five meters of fabric folded and wrapped just so). With fancy hair and red lipstick popping (in true Nepali fashion), we hopped on a bus to drive an hour out of the city to the cable cars. Most of the women had never been there before and were ecstatic to try something new, fun, and adventurous. We spent the day as a family, enjoying beautiful Himalayan mountain views and plenty of delicious Nepali cuisine.

I felt so honored and privileged to be a part of BFANepal's 10-year celebration. After serving there for just under two years, it felt like a wildly extravagant blessing to see the flourishing fruit of so many others' labor. You see, that's the thing in the Kingdom of God; we all take turns planting seeds, watering saplings, and seeing the blossoming flowers of the fruit of our labor wherever God has us. An incredible number of Kingdom laborers had come and planted or watered the seeds at BFANepal throughout the past ten years, which brought us to a place of reflection and gratitude for God's faithfulness. As we spent time together reflecting as a family, there was an overwhelming theme of God's blessing and provision in their lives through the business.

It was obvious to me when I came into the business that there was a firm foundation of trust, love for each other, and a true sense of family among the staff. I didn't build that; I just got to enjoy it and water it. I got to enjoy what others had been watering. For example, one of our staff, whom we'll call Amara, was physically handicapped and unable to walk without assistance. She had a bicycle rickshaw that she pedaled with her hands to get to and from work each day. Her coworkers would help push her and help her navigate the tough roads, but it was a huge struggle for her, especially when the road to work was under construction for months at a time in the middle of monsoon season. But Amara persisted through the hardship. She continued to have faith that the Lord would heal her. And in the waiting, as the healing had not yet come, she also had faith for a scooter to help her get to and from work much easier. So, we at BFANepal joined her in faith and prayed that God would meet her needs and bless her richly.

During my time there, we were able to bless Amara with a three-wheeled scooter for her to use. She was absolutely in awe of God's goodness, and tears streamed down her face as she praised God for answered prayers. This is a woman who would have been thrown out and discarded by her family, but because of BFANepal, she had a family, a job, and a scooter to ensure safe travels. She has absolutely seen the goodness of God in the midst of struggles, and I felt so honored to walk alongside her in one of her growing seasons.

So, wherever you are in the Kingdom right now, I want to challenge you to keep planting those seeds, watering those saplings, or picking that fruit. God has a purpose for you in somebody's growing season!

Ponder with Jesus

What about you? Are you intentionally investing in God's Kingdom work? Are you planting seeds in the Kingdom? Or watering little saplings? Or are you enjoying the pleasure of seeing full fruit in someone else's life? God's Kingdom is one of growth. If we're not growing with God and investing in His Kingdom work, we are missing out! There's nothing in this world that will satisfy more than doing life with Jesus. And where Jesus goes, the fullness of life follows.

Stop and reflect with the Lord. Are you investing in His Kingdom here on earth? Ask the Lord to bring to mind two people for you to intentionally pour into in the coming days, weeks, and months. Then stop, look, and listen. If people come to mind, ask the Lord more questions, "Lord, what's one thing I can do this week to get started? How will I make the time? What if I'm scared?" Be honest with the Lord and have a conversation with Him. He isn't scared of your feelings. Spend some time communing with the Lord.

Chapter 27
Choosing Joy in All Circumstances

Rejoice always, pray continually, give thanks in all circumstances; for this is God's will for you in Christ Jesus.

~1 Thessalonians 5:16-18 NIV

Choosing joy is something God had been talking to me about for a few months. I then felt led to do a 40-day fast for multiple things—one was to seek the Lord for wisdom, direction, and anointing for freedom/inner healing ministry. Initially, the thought of fasting for forty days was overwhelming and terrifying. I have loved to eat for as long as I can remember, and the thought of being hungry for 40 days was almost unimaginable. But as I prayed for grace and sought the Lord for His direction, I felt confident that He would sustain me through it and that I should go for it.

Now, I'm sure you've heard of being "hangry"—you know, being so hungry it makes you angry? Well, if there's anything that makes me more emotionally unstable than being hungry, it's being tired. Feel free to verify this with my previous housemates, Luke and Steph. As a narcoleptic night-shift nurse, I don't even want to admit how many times I was tired to the point of tears while living under their roof. So, all this to say, I'm human. I get "hangry", and I get "teary tired".

So, in the natural, the thought of being so hungry I couldn't sleep, and therefore, so tired I could just cry, sounded like a recipe for disaster. Thankfully, God's ways are higher than our ways. Thankfully, because of Jesus, we have the freedom to choose joy in all circumstances. Regardless of how tired or hungry or what our circumstances tell us, we have a choice! So, for 40 days, I learned to trust God to always be enough. I learned to trust God when I was hungry. I learned to depend on God for energy when I was tired. I learned to lean into God for more and more grace in every moment of every day. And He showed up in incredible ways, granting me grace to not only survive but thrive through 40 days with no food.

Admittedly, the true test of choosing joy in all circumstances came on day number 40. I spent the last few days of the fast visiting BFANepal's remote branch office with our intern, Gina. (To get to this office, it's about a five-hour drive from Kathmandu on roads that would rival a Ford truck commercial.) So, we started the day by hiking down a mountain for over an hour. We then waited for our bus to leave. We eventually started the bus ride home, and I immediately realized it was going to be a LONG day. The 20+ year-old bus had ZERO suspension left, and the roads felt like nothing but boulders jarring us from side to side. Additionally, the seat in front of mine was broken, so my full-size backpacking backpack was not able to rest safely against the seat in front of me; instead, I needed to hold it vertically to prevent it from smashing the person in front of me. (This wouldn't be an issue, except the bus was rocking side to side like Noah's ark in the earth-cleansing storm.)

So anyway, we're barreling down the boulder-filled road at record speeds of 25-30 miles per hour while we try to keep ourselves in our seats without our backpacks smashing our neighbors. Did I mention my window was broken and was continually sliding open to invite dust clouds to roll in and fill our eyes (and ears and mouths) with dust? At this point, Gina and I looked at each other, laughed, and said, "Oh, Nepal, always an adventure!" And we kept smiles on our faces...for a while.

Then we arrived (in record time, I'm sure) at the next village, where we apparently needed to wait for more people to board. So, we sat and waited 20 to 30 minutes before taking off for the next village. We repeated this race and wait, race and wait countless times. I cannot express to you the amount of effort required to keep ourselves and our bags in our seats. I cannot express to you the speeds at which we rounded those mountain-curved roads while narrowly missing oncoming traffic. To say it was an adventure would be a dramatic understatement. But we attempted to remain positive...for the first couple of hours anyway.

Then things only got worse. As it was day 40 of my fast, somehow my stomach was growing in anticipation of the food it somehow knew to expect, so my stomach was grumbling. I was tired, the bus ride was unimaginably rough, and yet, I was attempting to enjoy listening to worship music and sermons via my headphones until the Nepali music on the bus was suddenly turned on and cranked up to just a few decibels below a spaceship taking off. At which point, I turned to Gina and mouthed, "Really?" (Because, you know, there wasn't a chance she could hear me over the blasting Nepali music). And I thought to myself, "Really God, now I can't even choose to worship You throughout this miserable ride?" And I heard that still, small whisper respond, *"But you can still choose joy, remember?"*

And so, I did. I chose to look out the window and just think to myself all the reasons I had to be thankful and joyful despite my truly miserable circumstances. And then, the guy in the seat right behind me started throwing up out the window. I rolled my eyes at God and thought, "Really, there's more?" But I knew what His response would be, *"Will you still choose joy?"* And so, I tried. My rear end was raw from sliding down the seat so many times, my arms were literally sore from attempting to guard my neighbors from my thrashing bag, and my eyes were so full of dust I could barely blink. I tried to keep my eyes fixed on Him—the King who chose to leave His pristine throne in Heaven to enter this dusty and dirty world full of bumpy roads and chaotic journeys. I tried to believe that my small five hours of "suffering" was nothing compared to the cross of Jesus, Paul's beatings, or Peter's imprisonment.

And I was reminded that regardless of my circumstances, because of Jesus and His birth, death, and resurrection, I at least have a choice! I can choose to focus on my miserable circumstances. I can choose to dwell on being far from family and friends, far from paved roads and buses with suspension and air conditioning, and far from comfortable and familiar. Or I can choose to be thankful and joyful because I have a personal relationship with the Savior of the world—my Savior who knows what it means to leave the comforts of home, take difficult journeys to difficult places, and make sacrifices for the sake of God's Kingdom. It's all about perspective.

Ponder with Jesus

So, what about you? What circumstances are you allowing to steal your joy? We have a choice, but it's just that—a freedom to choose. But the choice is yours to make. Will you choose joy? Ask God if there's an area or a circumstance in your life where you need to choose joy. Then stop, look, and listen. What is He saying?

Chapter 28
Pondering God's Favor

And Mary said, 'Behold, I am the servant of the Lord; let it be to me according to your word.' And the angel departed from her.

~Luke 1:38 ESV

It's incredible how when we pay attention to what God is saying, there's a richness and fullness to our life and our journey with Him. Throughout my time in Nepal, I constantly looked for God's fingerprints and learned to tune my ears to hear from Jesus. One year around Christmas time, instead of keeping my focus on Jesus alone, God turned my attention to Mary. So, let's talk a bit about Mary, the mother of Jesus. I think we can learn a few things from her story. Let's check out Luke 1:26-38 (NIV).

> *In the sixth month of Elizabeth's pregnancy, God sent the angel Gabriel to Nazareth, a town in Galilee, to a*

> *virgin pledged to be married to a man named Joseph, a descendant of David. The virgin's name was Mary. The angel went to her and said, "Greetings, you who are highly favored! The Lord is with you."*
>
> *Mary was greatly troubled at his words and wondered what kind of greeting this might be. But the angel said to her, "Do not be afraid, Mary; you have found favor with God. You will conceive and give birth to a son, and you are to call him Jesus. He will be great and will be called the Son of the Most High. The Lord God will give him the throne of his father David, and he will reign over Jacob's descendants forever; his kingdom will never end."*
>
> *"How will this be," Mary asked the angel, "since I am a virgin?"*
>
> *The angel answered, "The Holy Spirit will come on you, and the power of the Most High will overshadow you. So the holy one to be born will be called the Son of God. Even Elizabeth, your relative is going to have a child in her old age, and she who was said to be unable to conceive is in her sixth month. For no word from God will ever fail."*
>
> *"I am the Lord's servant," Mary answered. "Let it be to me according to your word." Then the angel left her.*

I can only imagine the thoughts racing through Mary's mind. This was not a common occurrence. This was not expected and anticipated. Mary wasn't anyone particularly famous. Nazareth wasn't a highly respected town. Maybe she was just doing the dishes, the laundry, or going out for a walk? We don't really know, but we know she was probably an average teenage woman who was engaged to be married. And out of nowhere, an angel appears and says, "Greetings! You who are highly favored, the Lord is with you!"

Who, me? Are you sure? Why me? Who am I? How can you be certain? Regardless of what she was thinking, she said, "How will this be?" And in this moment, God invites her to step from the natural into the supernatural, for no word from God will ever fail. His promises are absolutely true!

And what is Mary's response to this life-changing news? "May it be to me according to Your word." Yes, okay, I trust You, Lord. I believe Your promises are true. I trust that You know what you're doing. Even when, from my perspective, this looks absolutely impossible, I will trust that Your word will never fail.

In verse 45, it says that Mary's cousin, Elizabeth, was filled with the Holy Spirit and exclaimed, "Blessed is she who believed that there would be a fulfillment of what was spoken to her from the Lord."

Highly favored? So, what did God's favor look like in the coming years? Well, she was nearly divorced and even worse, she could've been stoned! But God protected her. Then she gave birth to her son far, far away from her family and mother and potential sisters—possibly all alone with Joseph or with strangers helping her. Then she, Joseph, and Jesus had to escape to be refugees in Egypt because the local king was trying to murder her child. Then, eventually, things settled down, and they moved back home for quite a while. But then, she ended up watching while her beloved

Son was murdered on a cross.

This doesn't seem like favor and blessing to me. But here we are, more than 2000 years later, and we're still talking about Mary, the mother of Jesus. She was able to witness miracles of every kind—beyond our wildest imagination. She had Jesus Christ, our Savior living in her home. She spent cool evenings at home snuggling the Savior of the world—our God and King! Can you even imagine?

Sometimes, God gives us a word or a promise to stand on and cling to because He knows things are about to get tough. God's favor and blessings sometimes come with a lot of pain and heartache. I can't imagine how tough those first few years were for Mary and Joseph. And I cannot imagine sitting and watching my Son while He hung on a cross. But because Mary gave God her "Yes," she was the mother of the Savior of the world!

As that year was coming to a close, I spent time seeking the Lord for words and promises for the upcoming year. As His humble servant, I wanted to offer myself up to be used by Him. I wanted to say, "Regardless of the pain, suffering, or heartache it may cause, 'May it be unto me according to Your word!'" I know I don't deserve to be used in God's plans and purposes, but I am honored and excited that He would choose to use even me. I trust that His promises are true and that "No word from God will ever fail."

Ponder with Jesus

Are you willing to say, "May it be to me according to Your word"? Even if it means pain, heartache, loss, difficult seasons with confusing outcomes? Are you willing to lay down your plans for whatever plot twist the Lord has in mind? You know my opinion.

He's worth it every time. I want others to be able to say of me, "Blessed is she who believed that there would be a fulfillment of what was spoken to her from the Lord." But what about you? You have to decide if He's worth it to you.

I don't know about you, but I don't want my life to be so ordinary that I could do it by my own strength. I want to be a part of something only God could do! What about you? Are you dreaming big enough? Or do you need to spend some time dreaming with God? Are you open to whatever adventure God wants to take you on? Or are you dead-set on the plans you have for your life, and you simply want God to bless them?

We miss out on so much when we are determined to do things our way. God's ways are always higher than our ways. Will you trust Him with your future? Spend some time journaling with the Lord. Write out your plans and dreams for the future. Then, lay them at the foot of the cross. If you can't, remember to pray, "Lord, please make me willing to be made willing to lay my heart's desires at the foot of the cross." He's worth it. And He's inviting you into more.

Chapter 29
God Always Trades Up

*And provide for those who grieve in Zion—
to bestow on them a crown of beauty
instead of ashes,
the oil of joy
instead of mourning,
and a garment of praise
instead of a spirit of despair.
They will be called oaks of righteousness,
a planting of the Lord
for the display of his splendor.*

~Isaiah 61:3 NIV

Another thing God taught me during my time in Nepal was that He always trades up. He gives us beauty for our ashes, freedom instead of bondage, and wealth instead of poverty. He gives us love instead of fear. He grants us forgiveness, not condemnation, and truth in place of the enemy's lies. And in every single circumstance, when we hand Him our fully surrendered lives, He hands us back a life of fullness that we never could have imagined.

I remember saying goodbye to my family before I left America. I remember physically laying down my one-year-old niece with tears gushing down my face. I felt like I was symbolically laying down the very thing that was most important to me—my friends and family. Those relationships were so dear to my heart, but God asked me to lay down EVERYTHING, and not just the things that were easy to lay down. The cost of following Jesus is a very real thing, but I was learning that God never asks us to lay things down without handing us something better. My relationship with Jesus, my perspective on life, my level of surrender, and my passion for His Kingdom would never be what it is today if I hadn't said yes to Him—at ANY cost.

During my final eight months in Nepal, God asked me to start stepping out in faith in a very new and different way. And if we're being honest, this request felt even harder than moving to Nepal. Over the previous six or eight months, God had started talking to me about inner healing prayer ministry. For those that are unfamiliar, it is basically a couple of hours of intentionally seeking the Lord with someone using prompted prayers to help them find freedom from lies they are believing, a breakthrough in an area where they are struggling to find victory, or asking the Holy Spirit to come and bring freedom where there is bondage or healing where there is pain. My calling to this ministry was even confirmed through a prophetic word from a complete stranger, so I knew without a doubt that God wanted to use me in freedom ministries.

So, with this clear calling, I sought the Lord through prayer, fasting, and educating myself through some reading and training DVDs. However, I still felt completely inadequate and uncertain about how to move forward. Then, one day, I felt God say, *"Erika, you have everything you need; just step out into freedom ministries."* So, I was honest and told God I didn't want to, and I didn't know how. He said, *"Offer to pray with MaryLou and Matt."* (MaryLou and Matt were two of my close friends in Nepal.) I pretended not to hear Him. Fear was winning, and I suddenly had one hundred reasons why I shouldn't have to obey.

So, for the next week or two, I avoided the topic of freedom ministries and pretended like all was well, but eventually, I was so angsty I knew God wasn't going to let me off the hook. So I repented of my delayed obedience and messaged my two friends to see if they were willing to pray together and see if God would show up. Each of them had prophetic words about breakthroughs in different areas, so I felt confident that God did want to bless them while also leading me in this new, scary adventure. Both of them responded immediately that they'd love to meet together, so we scheduled times to meet.

I prayed for God to take away my fear, and He traded me up for some courage and confidence in Him, and suddenly, I felt ready to step out in faith. So, we met and prayed together, and guess what? God totally showed up and enabled me to help guide each of them to receive more of God's truth, more of His freedom, and breakthroughs in areas where the battle had been long and exhausting. God is SO good!

Erika DeJonge

Ponder with Jesus

What is God calling you to lay down for Him? What in your life needs an upgrade? Give it to God, and I promise He'll give you something better in return! He always trades up! Is He asking you to step out in faith? Is there something you have felt nudged to do but just don't have the courage? Delayed obedience is disobedience. Repent of your delay, and take the next step now! He's worth it! Be honest with God about how you're feeling, and ask Him for His truth about the situation. Ask Him, "Jesus, what do I need to know in order to take this next step?" Or, "Jesus, what's the next step You want me to take?" Then stop, look, and listen. What are you seeing, hearing, or sensing? Then don't delay—just obey.

Chapter 30
Freedom From Striving

The Spirit of the Sovereign Lord is on me, because the Lord has anointed me to proclaim good news to the poor. He has sent me to bind up the brokenhearted, to proclaim freedom for the captives and release from darkness for the prisoners.

~Isaiah 61:1 NIV

For a season, God was teaching me about the freedom He wants for me in regard to time. As a human, I am very motivated by achieving, which is a great strength when you have much to accomplish. Sometimes, however, my greatest strength can become my greatest weakness. I quickly feel guilty if I'm reading a fiction book instead of one with a purpose. I strongly dislike watching TV or movies because it feels like I'm "wasting time." (Just ask Liv; she used to have to DRAG me away from Jesus' time to watch a movie with her on Friday nights.) All too often, I try to gain hypothetical "bonus points" with Jesus by using my high motivation to achieve.

I feel like if I just study the Word a bit more, work a bit harder at work, or just pray for one more hour, I can please Him just a little bit more, and He'll come a little closer. Thankfully, that's a huge lie. God loves me, is pleased with me, and will talk to me without me striving and achieving to earn His love!

Every moment of every day, I feel pressured to be intentional with my time. This isn't inherently bad, but I do feel like God was fathering me into a more freedom-filled lifestyle of love and adoration instead of service and striving. He doesn't want me to feel guilty for reading a book for pleasure. He doesn't want me to stress about performing or achieving things for His Kingdom. He wants me to know in my heart that He is equally pleased with me, whether I'm studying the Bible, serving at BFANepal, or resting at the pool with a friend. He delights in me; He is ravished by me—end of story. There is nothing I can do to make Him love me more or love me less.

One week, without much planning, Liv (my roommate, boss, friend, and travel buddy) and I took a quick trip to Singapore. I was amazed as Jesus taught me in a new way how He will continue to speak to me and draw near even when I'm relaxing and enjoying traveling the world.

God had been showing me how much He loves to spoil His children with blessings far beyond what I could ever ask or imagine. Let's be real. I was living on a missionary budget and didn't expect to live extravagantly. However, Jesus continued to shock me! We stayed with some other missionary friends who were staying in an extremely nice condo in Singapore. They said they were blessed to be a blessing, so we could stay with them for FREE! Additionally, they had friends with season passes to Gardens by the Bay, so we also saw some of the most popular sights of Singapore for FREE! It felt extravagant and like the rest we had needed for quite a while. Other than the plane tickets, we barely paid for anything. God loved me through rest, extravagance, time at the pool, time at the beach (my love language), and so much more. It was ridiculously clean (chewing gum is literally illegal in Singapore) and so, so orderly—such a novel concept when coming from dusty, dirty, chaotic Kathmandu. Even though we questioned if we should take the time away from the office, God was so quick to love on us in the details and grant us the rest and rejuvenation we needed.

God has continued to teach me more and more about the freedom He has for His children in EVERY area of life. He does not want us to be slaves to sin. He does not want us to carry burdens we were never meant to carry. He doesn't want us striving to meet unattainable expectations. He wants us to trust Him in every area of our lives so we can live in freedom while bringing His light and His Kingdom everywhere we go!

Ponder with Jesus

What about you? Do you know how to rest in Him? Or are you busy striving to please Him or others? Maybe you don't tend toward striving. What about your personality needs refinement? What do you struggle with? What is constantly driving you, bringing you stress, or weighing you down? Maybe it's striving, or maybe it's anxiety, fear of the future, need for approval from others, or desire to be right. There are countless personalities with different struggles for each one. I don't know your personal struggles, but Jesus does. What does Jesus want to free you from? Let's ask Him,

"Jesus, what do You want to free me from?" Then stop, look, and listen. Repent of anything negative He shows you, and then receive the freedom He offers you instead.

Bring to mind a heavy or stressful area of your life. (If the Lord's will is on earth as it is in heaven, we shouldn't have to carry stress here on earth. Can you picture being stressed out in heaven? Me neither.) There are many lies we believe and act like they're the truth. For example, I am unlovable; I need to act a certain way to be accepted; if people knew the real me, they wouldn't accept me; I need to earn love and affection; if they knew what I've done, they could never forgive me; I need to look or dress a certain way to be accepted; if I made more money, I would be happier. And there are a million more. Jesus knows what lies you've been functioning under, and He wants to bring you freedom! He came to set the captives free!

With the chaotic/stressful situation in mind, ask the Lord, "What lie am I believing that is causing me stress?" Then stop, look, and listen. If/when the Lord reveals a lie, go through the following steps.

1. I repent of partnering with the lie that _____.

2. I break all agreement with this lie right now in Jesus' name.

3. I forgive myself for partnering with this lie.

4. The lie that _____ no longer has any power in my life.

5. Jesus, I hand to you the lie that _____.

6. What truth do You want to give me in return?

7. Then stop, look, and listen. (He always trades up!)

8. Receive His truth into your heart and meditate on it. (Chew on it for a while, commit it to memory, and dwell on it.)

Chapter 31
Praying for Healing

And all the crowd sought to touch him, for power came out from him and healed them all.

~Luke 6:19 ESV

While Liv and I were in Singapore, we got to enjoy a wide variety of recreational activities. We felt like we were walking through the set of the movie "Crazy Rich Asians". Unfortunately, our host wasn't always able to join us on our walks around the bay because her knee had been swollen and painful for weeks.

Thankfully, Jesus is the perfect representation of the Father. It says so in Hebrews 1:3, "The Son is the radiance of God's glory and the exact representation of his being, sustaining all things by his powerful word. After he had provided purification for sins, he sat down at the right hand of the Majesty in heaven" (NIV). Jesus healed everyone who came to Him, as mentioned in Luke 6:19

and an assortment of other passages. Therefore, we can deduce that the Lord's will is for all to be healed. Jesus displays to us the Father. Jesus prayed, *"Your will be done on earth as it is in heaven"* (Matthew 6:10 ESV). Why would we believe that God wants us to live in bondage and sickness if His perfect representation healed all who came to Him?

When the disciples couldn't heal someone, they didn't create a false theology stating it was God's will for the person to suffer a little longer. They went directly to Jesus and asked Him what on earth happened. Why couldn't we heal the boy with the demonic spirit? (Matthew 17: 14-20).

I don't pretend to have all the answers on why some are healed, some suffer longer, and some die. In fact, I had gone forward at multiple different prayer services for healing from narcolepsy before I was finally healed. I don't know why I had to wait eight years for my healing to come. But I do know that 100% of the people we don't pray for don't get healed. And my prayer to success ratio is pretty poor, but I know more people have been healed than if I hadn't prayed at all. So, I believe strongly that we as believers should be praying for God to bring healing to the sick and hurting here and now. If Jesus taught His disciples to pray, "May Your kingdom come on earth as it is in heaven," I, too, want to pray for God's kingdom to come here now and not wait until I get to heaven for healing to come. I'm quite confident there will be no sickness in heaven, so I believe we can pray for a lot less sickness here and now.

So, before we left Singapore, Liv and I prayed for our host's knee to be healed. We asked Jesus to take away the pain and swelling.

And God miraculously healed her knee! All the fluid and pain left! Praise Jesus, our Healer! She even messaged me a few weeks later to thank us again for praying because she was still symptom-free. We can bring God's Kingdom everywhere we go—even on vacation, He loves to join in the fun.

Ponder with Jesus

What about you? Do you believe in miraculous healing? Have you been taught that miracles ended with the disciples? Have you ever considered that maybe miracles are still for today? What does the Bible say? No, not what have you been taught? What does scripture say? Matthew 10:8 says, "Heal the sick, raise the dead, cleanse those who have leprosy, drive out demons. Freely you have received; freely give" (NIV).

Spend some time with the Lord asking Him questions. Don't take my word for it. Follow the disciple's example. Go to the Lord and ask Him questions! "Jesus, are miracles for today? What stands in the way of healing today? What have I been taught that isn't from You? Lord, what truth do You want me to know today? Is there anything or anyone I need to pray for today?"

Chapter 32
I Am More Than Enough

Yahweh is my best friend and my shepherd. I always have more than enough. He offers a resting place for me in his luxurious love. His tracks take me to an oasis of peace near the quiet brook of bliss.

~Psalm 23:1-2 TPT

When I left for Nepal two-and-a-half years prior, I thought I had learned what it meant to lay it all down for Jesus. It turns out that sometimes you have to learn the same lesson more than once. Over my first two years in Nepal, Liv and I had really grown to love our little flat that we had made our home. We liked to call it our "refuge" because we could come home and escape the chaos of Kathmandu. Our flat was comfy, cozy, and not-so-overstimulating (in contrast to the loud, bright, noisy, dirty, trafficky, and, did I mention, loud city).

About six months prior to leaving Nepal, God asked me to lay down the comforts of home once again. Sometimes, we think we have completely open hands. I had told God countless times, "All I have and all I am is Yours, Lord!" But then He asked me to give up my flat, and my response was a teary-eyed, "Really God? Again? You want me to give up my home, refuge, and familiar, safe space again?" And for a full day, I knew what God was asking, but I refused to be happy about it. I knew in my heart of hearts that I would do whatever He said, but I have to admit, I was more than a little bit grumpy about it. I might've even thrown such a little tantrum that Liv eventually said, "Erika, it's okay, we just won't move!" Moving in Nepal was never convenient, and I was moving back to Holland in less than six months. Why on earth should I have to move again?

To make a long story short, Liv and I knew some other Americans working in Nepal who were heading home for a furlough for almost four months. They had a house and a dog that needed to be looked after in their absence. They asked if we'd be interested in helping them out, and we felt like God was prompting us to bless them. The timing worked out almost perfectly, with Liv planning to move in September anyway, but the idea of moving when we had a perfectly good flat seemed absolutely crazy to me. Ashamedly, I have to admit, I was NOT a happy little Jesus-follower that day.

Thankfully, I only let my three-year-old self put on a display for one day. The next morning, as I was praying about whether or not we should move, I felt God say, *It'll be worth it.* And then I felt my heart bursting with God's love for this family. I felt like God was showing me His heart for them, how much He loved and cared for them, and how He wanted to take care of their every need. Whenever I started to feel overwhelmed by the details and logistics of moving in two weeks, I would feel my heart bursting with love for this family that I barely knew. I knew that God was reminding me how much He loved them and wanted to meet their tangible needs (and how He had that same love for me as well).

Additionally, He was using this move to remind me that He is always enough! As I prepared to move to a new, unfamiliar house further away from everyone I knew and further away from all my normal grocery stores and veggie stands, I was reminded to depend only on HIM! The comforts of our cozy little flat with everything in its place were not what kept me sane in Nepal. It was only the Great I AM.

For Christmas, a friend had given me a prophetic word that had a phrase for each month of the year. The word for the moving month was the phrase, *"I AM more than enough."* As I re-read that word as the month came to a close, it solidified in my heart that no matter where I go in this world, no matter what comes at me, God has always been, is currently, and will always be enough! No flat can ever bring the comfort of our True Comforter. No convenience can compare to the peace that comes with full surrender to the Great I AM.

So, as I entered a season of transitions, I chose to trust that the Great I AM would always be enough in every season. He would be enough to get me through the next two weeks of busyness as we packed and moved everything we owned across town while also hosting visitors from out of town while also heading to a wedding out of town the day we were supposed to move. As 75% of my community left for the summer (including my three closest friends there), I also chose to trust that He is always enough—physically, spiritually, emotionally, and relationally.

And eventually, as it would come time to pack up and move back to America, I would again choose to trust that He is enough. He will always carry me through the transitions of life. He will always be faithful and will never leave or forsake me. And most importantly, the Great I AM will always be enough. And I will always remember that "I shall not be in want." (Psalm 23:1 TPT).

Ponder with Jesus

What about you? What are you holding on to just a little too tightly? Is there anything God is asking you to let go of? Is there anything that causes you to throw a temper tantrum? Anything you would get whiny about if Jesus asked you to lay it down on the altar? Anything you have yet to surrender? It could be living close to your family, your home, your job that is familiar and comfortable, living on two incomes, or your comfortable American lifestyle. I'm pretty sure we, as Christians, are not entitled to a life of comfort and ease. We're called to pick up our crosses and follow Jesus. But always remember, His promise is for you, too. He will always be Enough!

Spend some time with the Lord and ask Him if there's anything you need to put on the altar today. Ask, "Jesus, is there anything I'm holding onto a little too closely?" "What do I need to surrender more completely?" Then stop, look, and listen. Don't let the things of this world own you; lay them down at the foot of the cross and determine in your heart that the Great I AM will always be enough. If it doesn't feel true, ask the Lord to show you a picture that solidifies in your heart that He is more than enough in this season. Then cling to that truth and practice walking in it—Even if it feels hard. Jesus paid for you to live a life of freedom. Don't settle for anything less!

Chapter 33
He's a Good, Good Father

The name of the LORD is a strong tower; the righteous man runs into it and is safe.

~Proverbs 18:10 ESV

I like to picture a three-year-old demanding ice cream for breakfast. Sure, it tastes good, but it's not a good idea. As a parent, you know that, but as a three-year-old, life feels unfair like your world is caving in because you can't have it your way!?! I'll admit I felt the same way when Jesus asked me to move. I could not see how that could possibly be a good idea. No way. No how! I was comfortable right where I was. Thankfully, Jesus knew better.

Thankfully, God always trades up! As it turned out, the new house we were asked to look over was MUCH nicer than our old flat. God is just so funny. I won't deny I was not excited about moving. And admittedly, it took me a second to get on board with giving up my cozy flat to move across town, but God said, "*It will be worth it.*" And as always, He was right. Not only was our new house much, much bigger and nicer, but we also had paved streets with curbs, gutters, street lights, and neighborhood kids that played in the streets! We also had access to a gym and a pool! This may not sound like a big deal, but it was a dramatic step up from our previous neighborhood. I cannot even convey to you how much our new house felt like a gift straight from heaven. God continued to teach me that He is a God of more than enough, of wealth, of blessings, and of so much more than I could imagine.

God's got such a sense of humor. I was living on a missionary budget, but a few months prior, I was staying in a multi-million dollar condo for a week for free in Singapore and getting free tickets to the Gardens by the Bay. And then we moved into one of the nicest neighborhoods in Nepal—for free!?! God sure knows how to trade up! He's a good, good Father who loves to bless His children. God just continually astonished me with His faithfulness.

I know I've talked a lot about surrender thus far. But I just have to remind you Who we're surrendering to. We're surrendering to a good, good Father Who knows exactly what we need to grow into the sons and daughters He created us to be. He is a loving Father Who pushes us when He knows we're ready to grow. He protects us when He sees things coming that we're not prepared for. He comforts us when we fall flat on our faces. He encourages us to get up and try again. He blesses us richly as we learn to run with Him. He tests and challenges us to help strip away all the nasty habits we've developed. He speaks to us and guides and directs our paths because He sees the big picture and knows so much better what we need.

Ponder with Jesus

I don't know what season of life you're in. I don't know what you need. I don't know what you're struggling with, but I promise God wants to reveal more of Himself to you. In that season, I needed to know the Great I AM. The God that is always Enough. Maybe that's helpful to you, or maybe it doesn't speak to your heart right now. Jesus knows what your heart needs to hear, and God knows in what aspect of His character you need greater revelation.

So, ask Him. "Jesus, Who are You to me today?" Then stop, look, and listen. What do you hear, see, or sense? As He reveals more of Himself to you, stop and stare at His goodness. Worship Him for who He is and Who you are learning that He is. Maybe you're growing in revelation of Him as your Provider, Protector, Father, Friend, Master, Comforter, Humility, Wisdom, or a LONG list of other characteristics of God. Whatever you need Him to be today, worship Him as that.

Chapter 34
God Sees Our Every Need

But seek first the kingdom of God and his righteousness, and all these things will be added to you. Therefore do not be anxious about tomorrow, for tomorrow will be anxious for itself. Sufficient for the day is its own trouble.

~Matthew 6:33-34 ESV

As I neared the end of my time in Nepal, I had the pleasure of hosting a team from the Bethel School of Supernatural Ministry from Redding, California. They came for twelve days to love and serve the people of Kathmandu. They served with a wide variety of ministries in the city, but they were truly an answer to prayer for me personally. The team happened to be led by an inner-healing counselor from Bethel Church named Cyndi. She had been counseling and doing inner-healing ministry for the last twenty years. As God had been taking me on this journey toward inner-healing prayer ministry, I had asked Him for mentors or people to learn from, but I hadn't found anyone in Nepal to study under. He had asked me to just trust Him to show up each time, so I had been depending fully on Him and not my own capabilities.

But then God sent me someone from Bethel Church where they have a transformation center specializing in inner-healing prayer ministry. Cyndi taught two sessions on "Counseling Tools" and led a time of inner-healing with one of our ladies at BFANepal. It was such a blessing to be able to learn under someone that God had been using powerfully for over twenty years! And I didn't even have to fly halfway around the world to attend a conference. God brought her directly to me for free!

Sometimes, our anxiety of figuring it out on our own gets in the way of us trusting the Lord to provide for our every need as we walk with Him and pursue His Kingdom in our lives as it is in heaven. I could've slammed on the brakes and told Jesus I wouldn't move forward until He gave me someone to learn from. I could've refused to pray with anyone until I was able to go to a conference or meet with people doing what God wanted me to do. But I didn't. I trusted that where God guides, He provides. And so I stepped forward in faith, and the Lord provided exactly what I had been asking for—even above what I asked or imagined. He could've sent just anyone, but He chose to send an expert in the field that I was pursuing. He's just so good to us as we follow Him step by faith-filled step!

Ponder with Jesus

Are you seeking first the kingdom of God? I think sometimes, in the Christian faith, we feel entitled that God should bless us. But many times in the Bible, there are statements just like this one. *"But seek first the kingdom of God and his righteousness, and all these things will be added to you"* (Matthew 6:33-34 ESV). So often, we quote, "Do not be anxious about anything because the Lord cares for you" (1 Peter 5:7 TPT). But how often do you hear people quote the verses that call us to action? Are you seeking first the kingdom of God? Because THEN all these things will be added to you.

Psalm 37:4 is another one, "Delight yourself in the Lord, and he will give you the desires of your heart" (NASB). How often do we demand that the Lord give us the desires of our hearts while delighting ourselves in the things of this world? How often do we prioritize our families or the American dream and invite God to bless us? He says to delight yourself in the Lord first and foremost. That will automatically realign our desires with His desires. Then, it will be His great pleasure to grant us ALL the desires of our hearts! But first things first. Delight yourself in the Lord first. Seek first the Kingdom of God and His righteousness first! Then, all His blessings and provision will be poured out.

Living in habitual sin (think of socially acceptable sins like fear, anxiety, gossip, and unforgiveness, not just drugs, extramarital sex, and drunkenness), pursuing the things of this world, living distracted lives instead of purpose-filled lives. This is not the life we are called to. Grab your journal and ask the Lord to bring to mind anything that stands between you and seeking first His Kingdom. Write down whatever comes to mind. Then, ask the Lord how to scratch it out. What steps do you need to take to be able to rip out and shred up whatever is standing between you and pursuing His Kingdom on earth in your life as it is in heaven? Then do it!

Chapter 35
Praying With Intention

Therefore confess your sins to each other and pray for each other so that you may be healed. The prayer of a righteous person is powerful and effective.

~James 5:16 NIV

One exercise I loved to share during devotion time at BFANepal was the **ACTS** acronym. **Adoration. Confession. Thanksgiving. Supplication.** And because I can never let a quiet time go by without asking the Lord to speak, I add an extra "S" on the end so I can also ask Jesus to "**Speak**."

I was about to say that I don't have any incredible testimonies for this one. I just want to share this exercise because it's one of my favorites. But the reality is, I've been connecting intimately with God through this exercise since before middle school, and I think that's a pretty solid testimony. I think it was a fifth-grade lesson at school that taught the **ACTS** prayer, and it's just stuck with me. I don't use it every day or even every month, but when I want to sit down and have a really thorough prayer session, I quickly turn to the **ACTSS** exercise.

Sometimes, we sit down to pray and run out of things to say in two minutes. The **ACTSS** prayer helps remind us of different ways to pray, different things to talk to God about, and then, of course, to listen, too.

A is for **Adoration**. Imagine staring into God's eyes and worshiping Him for who He is. Adore Him for His holiness, majesty, and loveliness. Worship Him as your Good Shepherd, Father, Provider, Protector, Prince of Peace, Alpha and Omega, and anything else you can think of. Adore our Almighty God, and be sure to make it personal.

C is for **Confession**. How often do you sit down and confess your sins to God or anyone else? If you're anything like me, it's not at the top of your list most days. But we are called to confess our sins one to another and to come clean before the Lord. If we avoid confession, we are vulnerable to guilt and shame. The Holy Spirit will, of course, convict us, but if we are caught up in guilt and shame, we are more likely to run from God than to Him. Sometimes, I sit down and can't think of what to confess. I've learned this is a great place to practice listening. "Lord, please bring to mind any ways I've disappointed You or lived contrary to Your will." "Lord, please bring to mind anything in my life that saddens You." Then, confess anything He brings to mind. Repent means to turn and go another way. You don't want to sit down to confess the same sins every day/week/month. If you're stuck in a pattern of sin, ask the Lord, "What's the next step to walking away from this pattern of sin?" He's eager to help His children who want to turn from sin.

T is for **Thanksgiving**. This one is my favorite. Thank God for anything and everything you can think of. I love to thank Him for all the great people He's placed in my life. I love to thank God for His beautiful creation, the great experiences I've had, and the blessings He's given me. Literally, every good and perfect gift comes from God, so if you're thankful for anything, be thankful to God! He's the one that blessed you with it. Some days, thanksgiving is super easy, but if you're in the midst of a super painful season, thanksgiving can be a key to finding joy in your life. Even on the worst of days, we can practice gratitude, and it can help us see God's goodness instead of our own despair.

S is for **Supplication**. According to Google Dictionary, supplication is "The action of asking or begging for something earnestly or humbly." I feel like that's a pretty good picture of how we should present our requests to the Lord, asking earnestly and humbly, but some days, it feels more like begging or pleading. This part of prayer seems to come naturally to us. We have no problem asking the Lord to provide for our every need, to bless those who need Him most, or to be present in our own circumstances. I think our Daddy loves to be involved in our day-to-day lives. I know He knows what I need, but I think He wants me to ask for His help. It takes humility to admit we need help, and I believe we should approach His throne with humility and present our requests to God.

S is for **Speak**. "Speak, Lord, for Your servant is listening." (1 Samuel 3:10 AMP). You already know by now that I believe prayer should be two-way communication. We just spent four whole letters on us talking to God. Maybe He wants a turn to speak. You can take this letter to ask Him to speak into specific circumstances, or you can leave it open-ended. "Speak, for Your servant is listening." But then you actually have to sit and listen. So, you know the drill, stop, look, and listen. Then remember to obey.

Ponder with Jesus

So now it's your turn. Spend some time practicing the ACTSS prayer. You can put on worship music and practice one letter per song. Or you can grab your journal and make lists. You can practice it with a friend and pray out loud together. Or you can go for a walk and pray while you walk. I'm not too particular, and the Lord isn't either—He simply wants to talk with you, share with you, and hear your heart. Here's one tool to help guide your conversations. Try it out!

Chapter 36
Interview Time

For my thoughts are not your thoughts, neither are your ways my ways, declares the Lord. For as the heavens are higher than the earth, so are my ways higher than your ways and my thoughts than your thoughts.

~Isaiah 55:8-9 ESV

As a person who is task-oriented and thrives in logistics and details, I often got distracted by the day-to-day grind of office work and easily lost sight of the beautiful mission and vision of the company I was working for. BFANepal exists to provide employment opportunities for marginalized and previously exploited women in Nepal. We didn't focus on the women's past stories, and I still don't even know most of their histories because we are new creations in Christ, and we don't need to dwell on the past but can be confident in who we are in Christ.

With all that being said, I felt truly honored and privileged to be a part of the interview process as we looked to hire four new women into our family. As our Executive Director was in the States for six weeks, our HR manager and I were responsible for the interviewing and hiring process. This was truly exciting because it meant the business had been growing, and we were in a position to offer more jobs to more vulnerable women.

At BFANepal, we hired women based on need, not skill. So, although we interviewed a few women who had nearly completed their bachelor's degrees, we passed them up for women with little or no education, women who didn't feel safe at home, women who had literally no other options for income, and who didn't always know where their next meal was coming from.

In a season of preparing to leave BFANepal, it was difficult to hear about so many women in such tragic circumstances, but it was also a fresh reminder of why I had invested so passionately in the business for three years. Sometimes, our women felt so stable and secure to me, but the interview process was a powerful reminder that they hadn't always been safe, secure, and protected. But they were now safe and stable because they had a consistent job that provided a living wage and benefits. But even more than the physical provision, BFANepal provided a safe place where women felt loved, accepted, and protected just as they were. You cannot put a price tag on a loving, stable family, and that's what BFANepal was to our women—a family that provided safety, spoke identity, and empowered women to believe in themselves!

I am so humbled that God would choose to use me, a nurse from Holland, Michigan, to love and empower the vulnerable and exploited women of Nepal, but I guess it's not capability that God's looking for; it's availability.

Ponder with Jesus

Do you believe that God's ways are higher than your ways? Or do you believe that the plan you have laid out for your life is better than anything Jesus could offer you? I'd like to tell you that working for BFANepal for three years were some of the hardest, most challenging, most refining years of my life, but it also ruined me for anything ordinary. The joy and fulfillment I found in living a life filled with so much purpose, faith, adventure, and Jesus has forever raised my standards.

What about you? Are you content with an ordinary life? Or will you pursue Jesus above all else, lay your desires, comfort, and ease at the foot of the cross, and receive the extraordinary, supernatural, purpose-filled life He has in store for you?

Put some worship music on and spend some time worshiping the One Who made you, the One Who called you, and the One Who has extraordinary plans for your life. Then, ask Him what He's calling you to. Open your heart to WHATEVER He might share with you. He's patient in the process. He loves to father you into your destiny. He doesn't expect you to be perfect; He simply wants you to be willing to partner with Him. Do you dare ask what He made you for? Do you dare ask what He's calling you to? If not, ask for more courage and wisdom. He's quick to give both! And remember, He loves you, and He's so proud of you.

Chapter 37
A Surprise from
the Holy Spirit

Jesus gave them this answer: "Very truly I tell you, the Son can do nothing by himself; he can do only what he sees his Father doing, because whatever the Father does the Son also does."

~John 5:19 NIV

Sometimes, doing life with the Holy Spirit feels like a life hack. One role of my job at BFANepal was volunteer coordination, which meant I was in charge of hosting quite a few short-term teams that came through BFANepal. One week, we had four or five different teams come through, and I had a project that I was hoping to have a team come back to help with. One day, Liv and I discussed which team we wanted to come back to serve. We both agreed a particular team had a few people with skills we were really excited about. The next day, I planned to message them to invite them back, but before I even had the chance, a few of them showed up unannounced and asked if we needed help with anything!

Their leaders had left them alone with nothing but transportation money and instructions to ask the Holy Spirit for directions for the day. They felt led to come to BFANepal to ask if we needed anything. It was their day of going out in faith, just believing God would use them and provide for their needs. Nepali/Kingdom hospitality says we feed everyone who serves with us. So, they came to serve us, but they were blessed with free lunch on a day they didn't know where their next meal was coming from! How awesome is that?

God never ceases to astound me with how well He loves and provides for us. He sent exactly the people I needed to get the jobs done before I could even ask! He sent our favorite photographer to take product photos using our specific style, along with the most efficient and particular pamphlet folders to fold our 5000 pamphlets just the right way. As a detail-oriented person, I just love how detailed and intentional God is in His love for us. He didn't just send any of the teams; He sent the precise people I desired from the one team we had chosen to call back. So, I was blessed, BFANepal was blessed, and the team was blessed all because these four people decided to listen and obey!

Ponder with Jesus

What about you? Are you seeking to listen and obey each day? Imagine the adventures you could go on! Imagine the stories you could tell. Imagine the testimonies you could share if only you started to listen and obey every day of the week. Let's practice again. I just never get sick of His voice! Ask the Lord for marching orders for today. "Jesus, what's one thing You want me to do today?" Then, listen and obey. Do whatever He says, even if it sounds ridiculous. Just do it.

Chapter 38
An Epic Surprise

Every good and perfect gift is from above, coming down from the Father of the heavenly lights, who does not change like shifting shadows.

~James 1:17 NIV

My boss, roommate, and best friend in Nepal was Liv. We ended up doing life together for two years straight. We lived and worked together, went to Bible study together, and shared most of the same friends. We rarely spent more than two hours apart from each other and truly built a beautiful friendship throughout our time together in Nepal.

Liv challenged me constantly to seek hearing from the Lord through many different avenues. She was and is incredibly prophetic and hears so clearly from the Lord. If I would ever complain about not hearing from God, she would always tell me God's probably just trying to speak to me in a different way than I'm listening. She sees God's fingerprints everywhere and is quick to seek His input on any and every question in life. One time, she was sharing a story about asking Jesus for a birthday gift one year and how His gift to her was so special. I thought to myself, why haven't I ever thought of that? So, I asked Jesus for a birthday gift my last year in Nepal, and He sent me on a bonus trip home!

Matt and Heather were some of my very best friends in Nepal; they had definitely become like family. They had challenged my faith like never before and were there through all the ups and downs along the journey. When my missionary advocate, Megan, came to visit and love on me for ten days one summer, all my friends were jealous and joked about how they all wanted a "Megan" in their lives. Well, over time, I felt God leading me to be Matt and Heather's advocate to love and support them from a distance after I left Nepal. They were in Nepal independently and didn't have a strong sending church to intentionally support them emotionally, physically, and spiritually as they constantly poured themselves into Nepal.

One Friday night, I was leaving a game night at Matt and Heather's. It dawned on me that Heather's baby bump would turn into a full-fledged human while they were home in the States over the summer, and they were going to return to Nepal with a 4-year-old, 3-year-old, newborn, ten 50-pound suitcases, and carry-ons to supply a newborn with supplies for the 36-hour journey. I thought to myself, "They'd be crazy to attempt that on their own! Someone should help them!"

The next morning, during my quiet time, I felt like God said I should help them make the return trip to Nepal. I had money set aside from before I left as my "just in case" money. I had told God that I had set it aside for me, but I knew in my heart it was His money, and if He told me to spend it, I would, of course, give it away. (Most missionaries there had epic stories of that one time that God had them empty their bank account to zero.) I felt like God was telling me to give the money away, but I would get to enjoy it, too. I thought, no way! There's no way I get to go home early! Are You serious, God? Then I felt Him say, *"Happy Birthday, Erika."* And I just about exploded with pure, ecstatic joy!

After confirming with Matt and Heather (who, of course, immediately said yes), I called my brother, Luke, who convinced me I should surprise the rest of the family. I thought eight months was a crazy long time to keep that caliber of secret, so I told him he was nuts. He told me to pray about it. I asked God for a confirmation. That same week, as I talked to my mom on the phone, she said, and I quote, "Is there not a single good surprise left in the world?" And I thought, well, yes, there is... You just got yourself one heck of a surprise.

About ten days prior to takeoff, through another awesome series of God speaking and confirming things and working things out for my good, my flights were moved up 48 hours, and I hopped on a plane to surprise even more people. So, the Friday of Labor Day weekend, after 52 hours of travel, I popped out of a car to surprise my brother, sister-in-law, and their three kids and then went on to shock my parents and other brother's family in a restaurant up north as we began an epic Labor Day weekend as a family—shockingly all together on one continent.

During my quick ten days home, I met my new niece, snuggled another friend's new baby, met a new baby bump, and saw three new houses and two new cars. I had countless great conversations, snuggled all the children, and visited grandparents. I tubed down the river, worked out with my workout buddy, played volleyball, walked on the beach, sat around a campfire, ate more than my fair share of hamburgers, donuts, and other great American food, and just soaked up every moment with cherished friends and family that I hadn't seen in nearly two years.

I then joined Matt and Heather in Washington, D.C., for a lengthy journey back to Nepal with our twelve 50-pound suitcases, three carry-ons, two backpacks, one stroller, one car seat, a 4-year-old, a 3-year-old, and a newborn. One could say we had our hands full! The trip went incredibly well, and it was a joy to be able to meet their families, enjoy quality time with them, love them, and serve them as I transitioned from local friend to long-distance advocate.

But also, I just felt so loved by Jesus. I got to snuggle all the new babies a full month earlier than anticipated, I got to surprise my entire family (I just love surprises!), and I began processing what it would look like to move back to America a month before I moved back "home".

Ponder with Jesus

What about you? Have you ever asked Jesus for a birthday gift? What about a surprise? What about good gifts? We serve a good, good Father who loves to pour out His gifts upon His beloved children. I just love how God loves us in the little details of life but also with huge, extravagant blessings. Take a moment and ask the Lord to bless you this week with a gift that is clearly from Him. Ask

Him to make it blatantly obvious that it's from Him, so you'll know in your heart of hearts that He is loving you intentionally this week.

Then, here's the hard part. Pay attention this week for a blessing from Jesus. It could be a surprise day off, an encouraging word from a stranger, or an unexpected raise or bonus at work. It might be a physical blessing, a new friend, or a gift of the spirit. The options are endless when You're the Creator of the world. The challenge is for us to pay attention enough to notice when He's blessing us. So ask, and then be vigilant this week to take notice of what the Lord is doing! Be blessed, my friend!

Chapter 39
Hearing God's Voice

Come to me with your ears wide open. Listen, and you will find life. I will make an everlasting covenant with you. I will give you all the unfailing love I promised to David.

~Isaiah 55:3 NLT

As I prepared to leave BFANepal, I had been reflecting on my time there. As I pondered all the things I had learned, I decided if I could only take one thing with me from my time in Nepal, it would be learning to hear God's voice. I will forever be passionate about teaching people that God still speaks today. He wants to lead and guide us, and He doesn't want us walking around in confusion with no clear direction. He wants us to know Him and encounter Him in very real ways.

So, if that was the one thing I wanted to take with me, it was also the one thing I wanted to leave behind. Throughout my time at BFANepal, I led countless devotions on hearing God's voice, practicing the prophetic, and seeking the Lord for specific guidance. The women at BFANepal ranged from Hindus to baby Christians to mature Christians and everywhere in between. In a group of 25 to 30 people, it's often hard to know how much our words truly sink in. Many of our women couldn't read, but I believed if they could hear God speak truth right to their hearts, He could bring freedom, healing, and direction to each and every one of them!

As my time at BFANepal came to a close, one of our devotion times involved practicing the prophetic. Each of us was to ask the Lord for a picture, encouraging word, or Bible verse to give to someone. Then, once we had finished drawing our pictures/words, we would draw a name out of the hat and give our prophetic word to that person. It's awesome because we didn't know who the encouraging word was for, but God obviously knows the future and knew whose name we would draw.

It was so incredible to see all of our women engaging with the exercise and getting prophetic words to share with one another! I was already so excited and encouraged that I almost forgot that I would also receive an encouraging word. Then, one of our women came to share her picture with me, and I was absolutely shocked as her picture touched on three different things the Lord had been talking to me about! This was such a special moment for me as I felt like God was showing me that the women really had been growing in hearing God's voice. This had been one of my greatest prayers—for the women to encounter the Living God and to hear directly from Him. I was absolutely overjoyed by God's faithfulness and how He not only answered my prayers but also allowed me to see them answered before I left!

Ponder with Jesus

What about you? Have you grown in hearing God's voice throughout our journey together? Have you grown in your ability to listen, obey, or both? Reflect for a moment on how far you've come. Celebrate any victories. Mourn any missed opportunities. Then, ask God something that's been on your heart or mind recently. I'm not giving you any questions to ask today. Ask Him whatever you want. Then stop, look, and listen. And, of course, obey any new directions you receive.

Chapter 40
My Challenge to You

My sheep listen to my voice; I know them, and they follow me.

~John 10:27 NIV

So now we've come to the end of my journey through Nepal, but my desire to listen and obey didn't stay in Nepal—it came home with me. My prayer and challenge for you is that you take what you've learned on your journey through this book and continue to develop your ability to listen and obey the One who made you. I challenge you to set aside time each day to seek to hear God's voice. I'm convinced my life will never be the same because I went on a journey of learning to hear God speak. I hope and pray that someday you'll be able to say the same.

Will you grab some courage and take the time to listen and obey at any cost? I pray you will. I promise He's always worth it!

Erika DeJonge

Ponder with Jesus

Now, this might sound absolutely terrifying, but the only way to grow in this area is to keep practicing. Let's start practicing hearing the Lord's voice not only for ourselves but also to encourage others.

Let's play a little game. Write the names of four of your closest friends or family members on pieces of paper and throw them in a bowl. Then pray and ask the Lord to speak. Pray something like, "Father God, Jesus Christ, and Holy Spirit, I long to hear from You today. Please come and clear my mind of any distractions and speak to me. I cling to the truth that You want to speak to me today, and You have given me ears to hear. Please open the eyes and ears of my heart and help me see and hear from You. Please give me a word and/or picture to encourage my friend today."

Then stop, look, and listen. Often, the Lord will start speaking or showing you things even before you're done asking. Don't be surprised; He's eager to speak to you! Just receive it and don't doubt! Whatever you think you see, hear, or feel, just write it down or draw it out. You can always go back later and discern if it was you thinking or God speaking. Just write it down for now. And keep asking questions. If you see a picture but don't know what it is or why you're seeing it, just ask! He wants to communicate with you. Keep asking more questions.

When you're done, review what you've written down. Is it encouraging, uplifting, and edifying? If so, you should definitely share it with a friend!

Pick a name out of the bowl. Because Jesus is outside of time, He already knows who you are going to pick, so your encouraging word is for the person Jesus knows you'll choose today. So, call them today and let them know you were practicing hearing from the Lord and want to share an encouraging word with them. I said TODAY! Don't put it off until tomorrow—fear will only grow bigger over time. Just call them today.

Notice the language there: "I'm on a journey of trying to hear from the Lord. Can I share something encouraging with you?" Don't call your friend and say, "Thus saith the Lord..." There might be a time and a place for that, but I'm confident they are few and far between. Go humbly to your friend and ask for feedback. We should always leave others feeling loved, edified, and encouraged, not ashamed, condemned, or judged. (There is a place for offering godly correction and discipline in the church, but it's not during your baby steps of hearing from the Lord.) Ask your friend if what you shared was encouraging. It's possible they were just praying for encouragement, and you were their answer to prayer. It's possible they won't understand and will be caught off guard, but hopefully, as your friend, they will be gracious. Jesus rewards our steps of faith. I promise He's worth it. So, take a leap of faith and practice! Share your encouraging words and invite people along on the journey of learning to hear God's voice!

Bonus—You have three names left in the bowl to practice with the rest of the week.

Epilogue

Erika DeJonge now lives with her husband, Andy, their son, Logan, and their black lab, Abbie, in Fruitport, Michigan—just a hop, skip, and a jump away from the gorgeous beaches of Lake Michigan (where Jesus lives :). During her time in Nepal, she received a prophetic word that God had a place marker in her dreams, that while she was being a place marker in Nepal—holding a space for God's presence to reside—He had a place marker holding a spot for her dreams (dreams of becoming a wife and mother and having a home to invite others into). And long before she met her husband, Andy's "door was always open, and the food was always hot." So, if you're ever in the area, be sure to stop by for a cold beverage, warm meal, or Spirit-filled conversation. And, of course, may your walk with Jesus always be filled with adventure!

About the Author

Erika DeJonge graduated from the University of Michigan in 2012 and has worked as a nurse in multiple settings in Ohio and Michigan. Currently, she is a nurse in the ER and ICU in Muskegon, Michigan. She served as a missionary through Engedi, a church in Holland, Michigan, and returned to West Michigan in 2019 after serving three years in Nepal with Beauty For Ashes Nepal. She then listened and obeyed her way to her beloved husband, Andy, and their first child, Logan. She has served on Engedi's prayer ministry leadership team working to equip its prayer team to hear from the Lord as well as helping children learn to see and hear from God. Erika has an intimate friendship with Jesus which has led to a journey of hearing God's voice, experiencing His healing and breakthrough, and serving many others in their steps toward "the more" of God.

References

Chapter 13

Rachel Bondi, Blog post, Shared with permission.

Chapter 14

Bickle, M. (2014, February 14). Studies in the Song of Solomon (2014). Mikebickle.org. Retrieved December 5, 2023, from https://mikebickle.org/series/studies-in-the-song-of-solomon-2014/

Chapter 20

David Mosterd while on a KINGdom Story Project Biblical Study Tour. Shared with permission.

Chapter 23

Edwards, G. (2012). 100 Days in the Secret Place. Destiny Image.

Warren, R. (2002). The Purpose Driven Life. Zondervan.

Lawrence, B. (2013). Practicing the Presence of God. Independently Published.

Chapter 24

[YouTube]. (2018, October 2). REST SERIES PART ONE - Michael Miller [Video]. YouTube. https://www.youtube.com/watch?v=rn6QHPVrpHQ

Chapter 37

(n.d.). Supplication Definition. Google.

Made in the USA
Columbia, SC
17 October 2024